# Rising Up From Mental Slavery

## How to Unleash Your Infinite Potential

# Rising Up From Mental Slavery

## How to Unleash Your Infinite Potential

Katerina Cozias and Danielle Martins

Copyright © 2018
Katerina Cozias and Danielle Martins

All rights reserved. No part of this book may be reproduced or transmitted in any form or by any means without written permission of the publisher, except in the case of brief quotations embodied in critical articles and reviews.

This material has been written and published solely for educational purposes. The authors and the publisher shall have neither liability nor responsibility to any person or entity with respect to any loss, damage, or injury caused or alleged to be caused directly or indirectly by the information contained in this book.

Statements made and opinions expressed in this publication are those of the authors and do not necessarily reflect the views of the publisher or indicate an endorsement by the publisher.

ISBN: 979-8-218-39300-7

# **Praise for**
# Rising Up From Mental Slavery

"There are no limits for those who really want to step into their purpose in life. This book will show you that any time is the perfect time to start to live life as you want."

— Adriana Miranda,
*Brazilian Digital Fitness Influencer, over 60*
Instagram @adrianammiranda

"*Rising Up from Mental Slavery* is a must-read for anyone who has ever thought about making their life better."

— Ari Gronich,
Sports Performance Specialist and Bestselling Author

"Success is predictable if you know what determines it. This book offers some valuable tips that will challenge you to leap beyond your current comfort level. If you want to strengthen your life, your business and your effectiveness overall, you'll discover a great friend in this book. You'll probably want to recommend it to all your colleagues."

— Jim Britt,
13-time Bestselling Author and Top 20 Success Coach

"*Rising Up from Mental Slavery* helps you break down the mental hurdles in your life that are stopping you from living your infinite potential."

— Diana Dorell,
Bestselling Author of *The Dating Mirror*

"Are you feeling it may be time to pivot but you just don't know where or how to start? This book will help you gain clarity on your true life's mission."

— Adam Markel,
Forbes Featured Entrepreneur and
Bestselling Author of the book
*Pivot: The Art & Science of Reinventing Your Career and Life*

"*Rising Up from Mental Slavery* guides you through the inherent nature of living the human experience—the never-ending quest for self-expression and self-development."

— Dr. Charlie Webb,
Leading Expert in Optimizing Health

"This book provides steps anyone can follow! Its stories are inspirational and the how-to is spot on."

— Nioshi Jackson,
Music Producer and Talented Musician

"A powerful roadmap for living life before it's too late. If you have ever said to yourself, 'I wish I could have done...' now is the time to read *Rising up from Mental Slavery.*"

— September Dohrman,
President and CEO of *CEO Space International,*

"Don't look any further for your personal how-to guide to change. This is it!"

— Steven E. Schmitt,
Founder of *The Law of Positivity*

"Having been in the personal development industry worldwide for decades, an architected work that resonates as an authentic bridge for progression rarely emerges. *Rising up from Mental Slavery* will be your guiding light... read it and know you now have your path."

— Jim Lutes,
President of *Lutes International, Life by Design*

"The freedom you seek is inside of you and this book will help you discover how to live the life of your dreams."

— David Boufford,
Founder, *MrPositive.com*

"*Rising Up from Mental Slavery* will bring you to new heights. Katerina and Danielle are inspiring, and a living representation of resiliency and dedication."

— Lin Van Gelder,
Retired Business Professional

"Fast-moving and accessible. This book leads you to where you want to be."

— Pas Simpson,
Happiness Engineer and Author

"Katerina and Danielle give you the formula for creating a successful life. Through their well thought-out path, practical exercises and personal experiences, these two powerhouse women will guide you to stepping into an amazing life."

— Chris Wise,
CEO of *Wise Profits and Founder of The Evolved Alpha*

"If you're looking for something more from your life, *Rising Up From Mental Slavery* is your compass."

— Shannon Burnett-Gronich,
Event Producer, Author, and Publicity Expert

"*Rising Up From Mental Slavery* will inspire you to be all you are meant to be."

— Erik Peterson,
Music Producer, Singer and Songwriter

"There's nothing braver than living life guided by the heart. Listening to your inner voice helps you make wise decisions and find/fulfill your purpose. This book is a powerful tool in assisting you to find the courage to walk that path."

— Silvana Lages,
Brazilian Personal Branding Coach and
Specialist in Self-Empowerment and Reinvention

**From Danielle:**

*To MY BELOVED SON, Rafael Martins, and my husband, Ricardo Martins, who rock my world. You are true angels that the universe has sent to teach me what unconditional love is all about, while at the same time, giving me a beautiful sense of belonging.*

*To my first mentor and friend, Américo Vieira. You showed me the path that woke me up from my mental sleep. Without your invaluable support and constant effort that helped bring out the very best version of me, chances are that this book would not exist. I was blessed to have had our paths cross that day.*

*To my dearest friend, Leandro Gardini, thank you for having believed in me, and for your constant support which means the world to me. Just as you are a blessing in my life, dear friend, I hope that I can be a blessing in yours. I am truly grateful to have you in my life.*

*To my "partner in this life mission," Katerina Cozias. You have brought me more than simply friendship; you have brought us the opportunity to share our love and light with the world. For that, I thank you.*

**From Katerina:**

*To my sister Krina, my biggest supporter and champion. I thank you from the depths of my soul for your constant encouragement and love. You are the best friend a girl could ever ask for.*

*To my mentor and friend, Christos Livadas. Thank you for always being there when I needed you and for being the brother I never had.*

*To my parents, George and Vicky Cozias, who have shown me more love than I could ever know. I am so very blessed to have had you always in my corner.*

*To my "partner in this life mission," Danielle Martins. Thank you for sharing your vision with me and for inviting me to work with you on the compilation of this book. I hope that it will be an inspiration to many people for years to come.*

# CONTENTS

| | |
|---|---|
| Introduction | 17 |
| **WHAT'S HOLDING YOU BACK?** <br> Do you control your thoughts, or do your thoughts control you? | 19 |
| **DISPELLING LIMITING BELIEFS** <br> The sky is not the limit; your mind is. | 55 |
| **TAKE 100 PERCENT RESPONSIBILITY** <br> You have created your own circumstances, and only you have the power to change them. | 67 |
| **YOUR LIFE'S PURPOSE** <br> Do what makes you feel alive. | 81 |
| **BUILD YOUR VISION** <br> Let your imagination guide the way. | 95 |
| **THE LAW OF VIBRATION** <br> What you broadcast to the universe is what is reflected back to you. | 109 |
| **AWARENESS** <br> What do you notice around you? | 131 |

**YOUR INFINITE SOURCE OF SUPPLY**
When you deal with the Infinite,
never expect to get less
than what you offer. 145

**ATTITUDE — THE MAGIC WORD**
One of the greatest discoveries of human
behavior is your ability to determine
your own attitude. 163

**THE INFLUENCE OF MENTORS**
A mentor is someone who sees in you
something you cannot see in yourself. 175

**THE POWER OF MASTERMIND GROUPS**
Leverage the mind power of a team to help
you go further. 185

Conclusion 195

About the Authors 199

# Introduction

If you are holding this book, chances are you are looking for something more from your life.

For that, congratulate yourself. That is exactly the inherent nature of living the human experience—the never-ending, always-expanding quest for self-expression and self-development.

Perhaps you know deep down inside that you are capable of achieving more than what you are currently achieving. Do you feel an urge to expand your financial success, create a stronger romantic relationship, carve out a better work/life balance, or gain increased freedom to do what you want, when you want?

Perhaps deep inside you do, but you are asking yourself: *Am I capable? Can I really attain all the things I dream of attaining?* The answer to these questions is YES.

It's natural to want to become all you are capable of becoming, because an individual who does not desire that is not living life to its fullest potential. It is perfectly correct and absolutely expected that you should desire to become the best possible version of you.

That said, a question you might be asking is: *How?*

We have written this book with the aim of helping you answer that question. In almost all cases, if you are not achieving the results you want to achieve, across either one or several of the various areas of your life, chances are you are being held back by hurdles that are more mental than they are physical. *Rising Up From Mental Slavery: How to Unleash Your Infinite Potential* is aimed at doing just that: assisting you in tuning to, and unleashing, your infinite potential.

There is no greater good you can render the universe or humanity than to make the very most of yourself, to become the You—the true, shining, magnificent You—that You were always intended to become.

There is an abundance of opportunity for anyone who can step out of his or her comfort zone and align with his or her true self. Know that you are a great living presence, always moving inherently forward toward more.

Together we will explain and explore many of the philosophies, paradigms, and thought patterns that might be keeping you limited, keeping you from becoming all that you can be. And together, we will explore ways to overcome these limits.

So, get ready and be excited. For there are so many amazing experiences just waiting for you to step up and live them!

# 1

# What's Holding You Back?

## DO YOU CONTROL YOUR THOUGHTS, OR DO YOUR THOUGHTS CONTROL YOU?

It's common to hear people complain about perceived limitations: from issues with their health to challenges in their relationships, from financial concerns to insecurities around the lack of formal education or successful career progression. On the other hand, others seem to thrive even during tough times. Think about it: we have all met highly educated people who seemingly have all the inherent tools to accomplish great things in life yet are achieving very little; while at the same time, there are others who on paper may not have these same credentials, but who are knocking their goals out of the park with win after win.

Perhaps you wonder: *How is this possible?*

*Shouldn't formal education be enough to help ensure success?*

*And if so, how can others who do not hold a university or higher education degree be so successful?*

Why do so many people finish formal schooling yet never achieve the professional success they thought they would? Why? Because upon graduation, perhaps they strove for that entry-level dream job but never managed to land it. After many failed attempts and much frustration, perhaps they then ended up compromising their own desires and simply took the next opportunity that presented itself—even if that opportunity had nothing to do with the career path they had originally wanted to pursue. Out of desperation, perhaps they agreed to take a job with a company they never had any interest in working for and found themselves doing things they never really had any interest in doing. After some time, perhaps they felt that they had lost control of the direction of their own lives.

Perhaps some of these people then decided to try their hand at entrepreneurship. Some succeeded, but many simply didn't. Little by little, their dreams of living an abundant life started to fade, and they became more and more convinced that they could not do anything to change their present circumstance. They now find themselves living day-by-day, paycheck to paycheck. They may have thoughts of grandeur still tucked away in the recesses of their minds, but they anchor to nothing concrete—no goals, no purpose—and over time, they have simply begun to believe that success, happiness, abundance, and fulfillment are privileges of the few. They feel like a lone cork bobbing in the ocean: subject to all sorts of winds, currents, and challenges levied on them by the mean outer world.

Many will agree that education is important, but in most educational systems, schools simply focus on teaching their students facts and figures, rewarding those who manage to best memorize those facts and figures. Most school systems simply don't go a level deeper, don't take the time to teach their students how to tap into the incredible power of their minds and their emotions in a way that can lead, truly lead, them to the creation of the life of their dreams.

How is it possible that almost 90 percent of all the money on this planet is held by only 9 percent of the world's population?[1] Why does only such a small and disproportionate share of the human race seem to enjoy *the finer things* in life? There is a reason for this, and many of the successful people are aware of what it is. But because it is so simple, it remains largely misunderstood and often unrecognized and unrespected by the masses.

We are living in the most expansive era in human history. Incredible amounts of data are now available to most, accessible with the simple touch of a button. The arrival of the internet has blown open people's access to

---

1    inequality.org/facts/global-inequality/

information. How many people are learning new things simply by searching the internet? How many deals and business transactions are conducted without the need of in-person meetings? How many possibilities have opened up because of the digital age? Yet, so many are still missing out on leveraging many of these possibilities.

Why some succeed while others don't is a topic that has been explored by the greatest philosophers in history. The answer? Well, it is quite simple. So surprisingly simple that perhaps this explains why it goes ignored by the masses:

> *A man's life is what his thoughts make of it.*
> ~ Marcus Aurelius

Thought. And the power of thoughts. It really is this simple. Most people don't recognize the importance of *thoughts*. They don't realize that they have the power to choose what they want to think and thus become who they really want to become in order to achieve all the things they really want to achieve.

Success has nothing to do with formal education and even less to do with chronological age. Success is connected with the ability to believe—to believe that *you can be, do, and have* anything you set your mind to do. Through the power of thought, you have access to the infinite potential that lies within you.

*Whatever the mind can conceive and believe, the mind can achieve.*

~ Napoleon Hill

Now first, let's clarify that *success* has many different connotations, depending on how you define it. Neither Mother Teresa nor Mahatma Gandhi were considered *financially* successful, yet few would deny that they were *influentially* successful. They lived out their respective missions, impacting millions of people along the way.

If you are a teacher, success may mean expanding your reach and traveling to a country in need to teach as many children as you can while giving those children the hope of a brighter future. If you are an entrepreneur, it could mean creating multiple streams of passive income and spending time working location free, learning from different cultures along the way.

For us, the definition of success is waking up every morning and living a life that we love.

Don't bend to others' definition of success. Don't feel pressured to follow the crowd. If you do, recognize that you are likely doing so because you were inadvertently trained to do so. Think about it: from the day you were born, you have been environmentally programmed and conditioned.

For example, the language spoken by the people who raised you became the linguistic way you expressed yourself. The ideas and ways of thinking that belonged to your immediate caregivers were transferred to you as a child. Their ideas shaped your perception of the world. The family culture, the food you ate, the clothes you wore, and even the thoughts you thought were passed down from your family and immediate societal influences.

In this same vein, the limiting beliefs you hold have been passed on to you by the people who influenced you as a child: parents, teachers, the media. The perceptions you hold today around what you are capable of achieving and how big you are allowed to dream have been largely molded by the thought patterns of those immediate, early influencers.

Call them *paradigms, mental conditioning, internal programming, personal philosophies* or *individual stories*: these thought patterns have shaped your world.

Early mental conditioning around a group of ideas, impressions, and beliefs can be likened to the software found in a computer. These beliefs are deeply logged in your mind and have the power to control almost all your habitual behavioral patterns. We each have our own set of mental conditionings, and the way each of us thinks, feels, and acts on a day-to-day basis is largely determined by them.

And so, what we need you to know is that if you want to create the life you truly desire, you must first develop an understanding of how such mental programming affects you at a deep level.

**Your mental programming controls your thinking:** Thus, you will inevitably have the tendency to choose thoughts and ideas that are in harmony with this programming. If your mental programming is largely positive, you will think positively; if it's negative, you will tend to think negatively.

**Your mental programming controls your feelings:** The thoughts you choose cause you to act according to how you feel because you are emotionally involved with them: good thoughts cause you to feel good, uplifted, happy—just like negative thoughts cause you to feel anxious, fearful, and stressed.

**Your mental programming controls your logic:** Too often many feel limited by what other people feel is logical. But at what cost? Do you think people believed the Wright Brothers were being logical in their persistence to get their flying machine off the ground? Yet, it was just that illogical thinking that helped to change the course of human history forever.

**Your mental programming controls your perception:** The way you perceive events in your life is directly determined by the dominant group of beliefs that reside in your subconscious mind. Raymond Holliwell makes this point well in his impactful book, *Working with the Law*, "More defeats and failures are due to mental blindness than to moral deviations" (BN publishing, 2008). A map is only a graphic representation of a place; it's not the place itself. A person who has been raised in a small town may think that a big city is too busy, dirty, loud; on the other hand, someone who has been raised in a big city might not feel comfortable with the stillness of a small town. But the reality is the small city is not too quiet, nor is the big city too loud. Rather, it is simply an individual's perception that makes it so.

**Your mental programming controls your actions:** As your thoughts are chosen according to your mental conditioning, these thoughts will lead you to rationalize, perceive, and feel things which are in alignment with it. In turn, your actions will be determined by these thoughts, and the actions will inevitably have direct consequences on the decisions you make, as well as on the results that ensue.

For example, if you feel powerful and confident in any given moment, you are more likely to take on greater challenges in a way that will lead you closer to your dreams and desires. If, however, you find yourself in a place where you lack self-confidence or feel you are not capable of pushing forward, you will probably not take much action and thus have a harder time producing the results you truly desire.

*Whether you think you can or you think you can't, either way, you are right.*

~ Henry Ford

If you are not satisfied with the outcome you are getting in any particular area of your life, understand that it is likely due to the mental conditioning that is controlling you. Unfortunately, for most people, that mental conditioning is producing results contrary to the ones they tell themselves they desire.

Indecision, procrastination, laziness, fear, lack of confidence, lack of courage, and lack of discipline are some examples of limiting mental programming. Consider this saying—often attributed to Albert Einstein—*it is absolutely useless to try and change your current situation by fighting your current reality.* You cannot change the effect if you are not first aware of the cause.

If you are experiencing financial difficulties, for example, an important step to take is to explore your mental conditioning regarding money.

How many times have you heard expressions, such as:

- *Money doesn't grow on trees.*
- *If someone is rich, it's because he has no integrity.*
- *Rich people don't go to heaven.*
- *It's better to be poor and honest than rich and dishonest.*

People who have been raised hearing these kinds of phrases will likely experience difficulty earning and keeping large sums of money. Unless they consciously start to change the mental conditioning around their thoughts toward money, monetary wealth will be practically impossible to achieve.

In another example, someone who has been raised in an environment where people drag each other down with negative self-talk may, in time, start to believe that they themselves are not intelligent or capable.

Much of today's mainstream media is guilty of broadcasting negative news. The result? When you watch, hear, or listen to mainstream media, you may start to feel apprehensive and paranoid, and thus begin to perceive a world where fear, violence, and insecurity ensue. In the same vein, when you become emotionally involved with a thought or an idea, this thought or idea is impressed onto your subconscious mind. It shapes your personality and thus becomes part of your mental programming.

The good news is that mental programming is nothing more than a reflection of the sum of your habitual thoughts and behaviors. These habitual thoughts can be changed, and changed for the better. Your habits are expressed in the way you act. Often, habits are subconscious. You don't need to be aware of them in order to act according to them. For example, most of us tend to put on our shoes starting with the same foot out of habit. This habit has simply been impressed onto the subconscious mind.

Your mental programming or mental conditioning can be likened to a thermostat. Successful people have their *success thermostat* set to keep them winning. Proactivity, decisiveness, commitment, enthusiasm, self-confidence, courage, and discipline are examples of the settings reflected on a successful person's thermostat.

Thus, winning can become a habit.

Winners are more likely to take risks because they are aware that although nothing is ever 100 percent guaranteed, believing they can win will bring them into closer alignment with winning and other winners. And winners help other winners achieve their goals because they are in a harmonious state of mind; they each respectively know how to create the circumstances required to more successfully achieve what they want to achieve.

Even if that person fails—and nobody is free of the risk of failing in this life—a successful person will be more likely to seek alternative opportunities to once again strive for the top because their very mindset or success thermostat is set to *win*. Since they are programmed to succeed, they will keep themselves focused on looking for opportunities and solutions instead of allowing their mind to be occupied with doubt.

In contrast, many people's thermostats are set on a lower standard of achievement, resigning them to a life of discontent and limitation. These people rarely see the opportunity behind a challenge, and they almost never seek to create their own opportunities. Often, if an opportunity does appear, shining brightly in a way that wants to be noticed, these people simply discount it, lacking the belief that this opportunity was intended for them in the first place.

It's precisely this type of negative mental programming that ensures they don't get off course and keeps them limited!

Picture the thermostat in your home on a very cold day. Let's say it is set at 24°C (75°F). When the temperature drops below that metric, the thermostat will instruct the furnace to start generating heat, which will in turn start to raise the room's temperature. When the thermostat detects that it has reached the desired 24°C, the device will stop generating any additional heat. However, after some time, the temperature in the house will once again start to drop. And so, before the room gets too cold, the thermostat will again prompt the furnace to start generating heat, and the temperature will once again begin to rise toward the desired 24°C. The system will always auto-adjust back to its original setting.

A successful person's internal thermostat works precisely the same way. Because the indicator is set to the designated outcome of *win*, their internal programming will do whatever it must to keep winning. When something goes wrong—when there's a deviation in this winning pattern—their internal thermostat will adjust accordingly to ensure it does whatever it needs to do in order to get them back onto that winning track.

Everyone's internal thermostat works exactly the same way; unfortunately, the average person's thermostat is, more often than not, set to keep them losing, not winning.

*To ignore the power of paradigms to influence your judgment is to put yourself at significant risk when exploring the future.*

*To be able to shape your future, you have to be ready and able to change your paradigms.*

~ Joel Barker

So, if you have tried hard to change a circumstance without success, it's time to identify the proverbial temperature to which your internal thermostat is set.

Remember, you are not a victim of circumstance. Rather, you created the circumstance. Everything you are facing right now, positive or negative, is a reflection of your own thought patterns, choices, and decisions. The decisions you have made, whether consciously or unconsciously, have been based on your internal thermostat or mental conditioning. Whether you realize it or not, you choose thoughts that are in harmony with your programming. Those thoughts, in turn, cause you to feel a certain way. Based on the way you feel, you are then moved into action.

And it is the combination of your actions that create your reality.

Wealth or poverty, health or sickness, happiness or sadness, good relationships or bad, accomplishment or the lack of—everything in your life is reflective of your own internal mental programming.

And so, it is important to identify which aspects of your life you want to change, and to then look to understand **what mental programming is holding you back** from getting what you want.

There are only two ways your mental programming came to be set:

- Through a traumatic past event which had a dramatic impact on your life *or*

- Through the repetition of thoughts, ideas, and actions that became imprinted onto your subconscious mind

Most people don't realize that it's not your conscious mind that determines the way you deal with daily situations. Rather, it's your subconscious mind, also known as your *emotional mind,* that moves you into action—or not.

You can, and must, choose your thoughts on a conscious level through your conscious mind, but it's the thoughts, patterns, and beliefs that are imprinted onto your emotional mind that actually control whether or not you will move into action. In other words: your actions are dictated by your emotions.

When you were a baby, your subconscious mind was receptive to all the information being directed toward you. As a baby, you had no ability to analyze or reject anything because your reasoning faculties were not yet formed. And so, influential thoughts from the people and things around you were simply absorbed directly into your subconscious mind.

After a certain age, the psychic barrier was formed between your conscious and subconscious mind, and you started to garner the ability to consciously accept or reject thoughts and ideas. But by then, the tendency was for you to opt to choose the thoughts and ideas that were already in harmony with your early mental programming.

Pursuant to this, there are only two known ways of transforming negative programming into positive programming, and they are exactly the same as the items above:

- Through a traumatic event which will have a dramatic impact on your life *or*
- Through the repetition of thoughts, ideas, and actions that become imprinted onto your subconscious mind

As a human being you have the ability to use your conscious mind to either accept or reject thoughts and ideas. Negative programming, the kind that holds you back or limits your ability to grow, needs to be re-categorized as obsolete information: if a thought no longer serves you, you must get rid of it. And the only way to get rid of it is by imprinting the opposite idea onto your subconscious mind.

Let's consider some examples of thought programming that, as you grew older, became obsolete of their own accord and therefore discarded. As a child, you may have heard comments, such as:

- *Never cross the street unless accompanied by an adult.*
- *If you don't tend to your toys, they are going to be angry with you.*
- *Leave a cup of milk and some cookies for Santa Claus.*

These are examples of thoughts you may have once held as true, but over time, no longer served you. And so, you simply made up your mind to release or replace them.

As an exercise now, take a moment and identify some of the types of statements you grew up hearing as a child. How many of them have you since discarded or mentally re-filed as obsolete? Which of those beliefs no longer holds any value for your current self?

Examples of ideas and concepts—or mental programming—that are often passed down from generation to generation, entering your subconscious mind without you being consciously aware of them, include beliefs around money, sentiments around intellect, and perceptions of what constitutes beauty. Many people go through life oblivious to the fact that they are currently making decisions based on thoughts and ideas that aren't even really theirs.

It is important to know that nothing is inherently good or bad; rather, it simply just is. What shapes your reality is your perception—how you choose to view the situation and whether you choose to put a positive or a negative moniker on it. Let's look at this concept through an analogy. We can liken thought to a knife. A knife is neither inherently good nor inherently bad. Depending on how it is used, it can either innocently spread butter or be used to viciously kill someone. Thought can either be used to serve you or used to sabotage you.

Moneymaking is a practical step toward wealth creation, but wealth creation itself is a challenge for a lot of people. Many times, it's your own subconscious beliefs around money that create resistance to attaining it. Pervasive negative thoughts and beliefs around money are often passed down through generations.

People are raised in environments where it's common to hear statements, such as:

- *Money is the root of all evil.*
- *Rich people are miserable.*
- *Money doesn't buy happiness.*

On the flip side, others grow up in environments where the opposite beliefs around money hold true:

- *Money is easy to earn.*
- *Money is fun to make.*
- *Money allows freedom.*

At the end of the day, money, like the knife from our earlier example, is neither good nor bad. Its successful attainment can be attributed to the type of beliefs you hold around it.

The same concept can be applied to the perception of your own intellect. Because so many negative ideologies tend to be passed down from generation to generation, unsuccessful people often believe that their poor financial results are due to their own lack of intellectual capacities. When instead, the truth is that their poor financial results are simply a reflection of their habitual thought patterns, many of which are due to negative mental programming.

If you were raised being told that you were not enough, take a moment to consider whether you still believe that. How has this belief served you over time? If it hasn't served you—which it likely hasn't—it's time to *get rid of it!*

Understand that the people you heard that from had likely measured your abilities based on what they perceived their own capabilities to be. Your ability to achieve has nothing to do with their perception of what you can and can't do. Their opinion of you is in no way a determinant of your true ability.

If you want to become the greatest version of you, you must start today to build up your own self-talk. In order to truly grow, you must dare to move out of your comfort zone with respect to your own thought processes. You have infinite potential inside you. You are not here by accident. If there is a burning desire you hold in your heart, know that it can be attained. You simply need to embed into your subconscious the belief you can do and achieve what you want to achieve.

*It's not who you are that holds you back, it's who you think you are not.*
~ Denis Waitley

Let's explore society's beauty standards and how these differ depending in which part of the world you find yourself. If you travel from one city to another, from one country to the next, you will find disparities in the types of physical traits people consider beautiful. But what others think shouldn't matter. The question you should ask yourself is: *What do I consider beautiful?*

Don't allow yourself to become influenced by the thoughts and beauty standards set by others. Love yourself the way you are: your curves or your thin figure; your straight or your curly hair; your freckles or your lack thereof. Remember that your physical appearance is simply one aspect of you. True beauty lies beneath the surface and is made up of a composite of your mental attitude, your actions, and the way you impact other people's lives. Embrace your uniqueness.

This is what the world needs: unique individuals who know how special they are and who hold strong, inspiring values and visions which they embrace and, in turn, share with humanity. It is crucial to become aware of your dominant mental programming, especially if it tends to be predominantly negative. Negative programming does not serve you. It keeps you feeling limited, incapable, and unworthy.

To change negative programming or alter poor habitual thought patterns, you must first recognize them. Once identified, it is only through constant repetition of new, more desired beliefs and thoughts that you will begin to imprint different, more desired beliefs onto your subconscious mind. Through repetition, the new beliefs will eventually become your dominant thoughts and positively affect your habitual behavior.

By taking action based on these new thoughts, new habitual behaviors will begin to imprint themselves onto your subconscious mind. In time, those new habits and behaviors will start to reshape your personality, and you will start to notice positive changes taking place in your life.

Identify your limiting beliefs and start to reprogram your thoughts and actions:

- Is your shyness holding you back? Replace thoughts of *I am shy and can't easily meet people* with repetitive thoughts of *I meet people easily and effortlessly.*
- Is your tendency to procrastinate holding you back? Replace thoughts of *I can't be bothered* or *I'll do it tomorrow* with repetitive thoughts of *I get my tasks done immediately and on time.*
- Is your tendency to complain serving you? Replace thoughts of *everything sucks* with repetitive thoughts of *I am so grateful for the opportunity to enjoy this experience.*

You have the power to control your own thinking. And the lack of organized and highly directed thoughts and actions leads to a messy life.

Fire, if left unattended, can be destructive. When properly directed, however, fire can be harnessed for good. Life is not much different: when you are not control of your thoughts, your life is like a raging wildfire—out of control, with no direction and no definite course. In this state, is it any wonder you are not achieving the results you want?

*Thoughts* cause you to feel, your *feelings* cause you to act, and your *actions* produce your reality.

Doubtful? Think of a sad moment you experienced in the past, such as the loss of a loved one. How does your body react to this thought? Do you feel a knot in your throat? Do your eyes flood with tears?

Now, think of something exciting: the birth of your child, the attainment of that goal, even the expectation of something you think will bring you the good you desire. How is your body reacting now? Are there butterflies in your stomach? Is there a huge, silly smile taking over your face?

You really can control your feelings by controlling your thoughts, and the way you feel will cause you to act according to those feelings. The totality and efficacy of your actions make up the results you see in your life. This is why it is so important to reinforce positive self-talk: the way you talk to yourself causes you to feel a certain way, and that feeling directly relates to the energy you put into action items.

If you think in negative terms about yourself, you will feel negatively about yourself. Then, your negative feelings will cause negative actions, which will lead to negative results.

Imagine that one day you are feeling a bit down, doubting your abilities and capacities. Let's then suppose that a friend comes to you with an opportunity, but because you are having a bad day, your internal dialogue is cluttered with negative self-chatter which may include thoughts, such as:

- *I am not good enough for this.*
- *I am not prepared.*
- *I can't do this now.*

Based on thoughts of fear, mistrust, and lack of self-confidence, you decline the offer. Had you been in a more positive state of mind, however, perhaps you would have explored the opportunity and your life would have improved.

*If you must doubt something, doubt your limits.*
~ Price Pritchett

Another name for this internal talk is *auto-suggestion*. Auto-suggestion is the repetition of thoughts and beliefs within your own mind, to your own self. Whatever thoughts and beliefs you choose to contemplate become imprinted onto your subconscious mind. These thoughts develop as part of your personality, and over time, they seek external expression.

One way people are exposed to and inadvertently accept negative concepts as truth is by not consciously recognizing all the subliminal messages directed at them via advertising, social networks, the media, influencers, and so on. Messages not of their own making are constantly bombarding people. Think about it: There are a lot of creative sayings circulating. Often, these sayings appear *cool* or *hip*, but how many of us question what these messages are actually relaying into the subconscious minds of the masses?

We see T-shirts for kids with phrases imprinted on them such as: BAD BOY or MEAN GIRL.

Adult wear shirts with quotes such as: EVERY GREAT IDEA I HAVE GETS ME IN TROUBLE, or NOT UNTIL I HAVE MY COFFEE, or I NEVER LIKED YOU. Sometimes there are photos with additional comments, such as LAZY PEOPLE ARE THE MOST INTELLIGENT, or SOMETIMES I WONDER TO MYSELF HOW DANGEROUS I WOULD BE IF I CARRIED A GUN?

These seemingly innocent statements are actually quite influential in that they have the power to affect our internal self-talk. Sarcastic remarks that appear cool and funny are being directed into the masses' subconscious minds with few people actually questioning how these statements affect them. Many of these types of statements perpetuate laziness, procrastination, lack of commitment, depression, and isolation as not only normalized but also as sought-after behaviors.

Consider this excerpt from Earl Nightingale's audio, *The Strangest Secret*, recorded in 1956:

> Some years ago, the late Nobel prize-winning Dr. Albert Schweitzer was asked by a reporter, "Doctor, what's wrong with men today?"
>
> The great doctor was silent a moment, and then he said, "Men simply don't think."

This comment is still relevant today.

In order to take back control of your own mind and your ability to think in a way that serves you, you must start questioning what society wants you to accept as normal. Messages such as these above go directly into your subconscious mind and re-shape your personality, influencing who you think you are or are not, and what you think you can or cannot accomplish.

It is not your conscious, reasoning mind that moves you into action; it is your subjective, subconscious, emotional mind. So, instead of being hard on yourself for your inability to move past your current circumstance, acknowledge that there is subconscious mental programming at play that may be holding you back. Replace this programming with the repetition of new, more effective thoughts and ideas.

> *People don't resist change. They resist being changed.*
> ~ Peter Senge

Know that it's never too late to change, and that when you change from within, life becomes magical.

# EXERCISE

The following questions are designed to help you identify and isolate thought patterns that may not be serving you. This is a self-evaluation exercise. The intention is for you to dig deep into your memories in order to bring past and unconscious details of thought and behavioral patterns to the surface. Once identified, attempt to find the correlation between your current behavior and your internal self-talk.

Take your time. Ideally it would be best to do this exercise in one sitting, but if you can't do it all at once, don't worry; the most important thing is that you do indeed complete the task. We've provided some leading questions and examples for you here.

1. For each category listed below, identify three areas that you feel could use some improvement.

    - Finances
    - Career
    - Health and Fitness
    - Social Relationships
    - Love Relationships
    - Parenting
    - Spirituality

2. Next, for each area you identified as needing improvement, identify what limiting belief you hold

around that topic. What thoughts or beliefs have you inadvertently absorbed from others that may not be serving you?

3. For each limiting belief, create a new, more positive belief. Forget what you currently believe to be true and ask yourself: *What do I want to believe?*

To get you started, let's do one together. Under the heading, *Finances,* let's begin with an area that could use improvement:

> *My monthly cash flow. I wish I could make more money than I'm making. I would like to increase my salary by 20 percent.*

Limiting beliefs:

- *I shouldn't ask for more money because money is evil.*
- *Money corrupts society.*
- *Those who have a lot of money are crooks.*

New beliefs:

- *I do a great job here at work and, as such, I feel confident asking for a raise.*
- *Money is simply energy. The more I have, the more goodness I can spread.*
- *People with money contribute to society and the betterment of all. I want to be one of those people.*

4. Once completed, take the time to read your new beliefs daily. Do this for ninety days. By repeating the new beliefs over and over, you will start to effectively reprogram your subconscious mind by replacing the previous detrimental beliefs with the new, more positive ones. In time, these new beliefs will imprint themselves onto your subconscious mind, and your thoughts will become an asset rather than a hindrance.

The more quickly and clearly you can identify what thoughts have been holding you back and replace them with thoughts that better serve you, the faster, more definitively things will change for the better.

New thoughts → new beliefs → new motivation → new actions → new results!

Know thyself. Conquer yourself and your own internal dialogue, and you will find that over time, many of the present challenges you are facing will dissipate, for understanding brings clarity and order to the mind.

# AUTHORS' PERSONAL EXPERIENCES

*Danielle*

My childhood was marked by the transmission of limiting mental conditioning and negative paradigms of those who raised me. Because I trusted the authority figures who passed these negative thoughts along to me, I never questioned the validity of the concepts. I simply accepted them as truth without recognizing the detrimental effects there were having on my life.

Although there are too many examples to touch on now, two of the main areas where exposure to wrong thought and limiting beliefs negatively affected me were with money and trust paradigms. Because of the way I was raised and the ideologies that were prevalent, I had a hard time trusting people and often trusted the wrong people.

I grew up with firm ideas about how people should interact, their relationships to each other, and their relationship to money.

I was raised hearing statements such as:

- *People can't be trusted.*

- *People with money are the worst kind of people.*
- *Rich people don't help people in need; they only help other rich people*

I believed money was evil and that you couldn't easily trust people. Under that mistaken thought paradigm, I used to feel terrible about myself when I would yearn for something more than just the ordinary life I was leading.

I was in a state of ambivalence, with part of me wanting to experience a more abundant life and the other part of me feeling that if I did, I would suffer. And I felt miserable. Because according to my mental paradigm, if I wanted to be rich, that meant I would become a bad person.

Despite my early thought conditioning, I was by nature always an expansive and altruistic person. Because of conditioning, however, I could never really trust anybody. The belief I held was that everybody who interacted with me was looking to take advantage of me in some way, especially those who had money. As you can imagine, my attempts at earning money or creating deep relationships in my life simply didn't work.

I used to feel unworthy when asking for the money I deserved when negotiating jobs or charging for services. Because of this, my financial situation never improved.

On one hand, the way I related to other people has always been beyond generous; on the other hand, I didn't trust people. When I did trust, they were the wrong people. I didn't have the emotional maturity to identify if someone genuinely liked me or not, so I rarely made the right choices when it came to choosing which people to spend time with. The more I was hurt, the more that pain validated the belief that people were not to be trusted.

However, when I became aware of the power of thought to influence outcomes, I finally understood that the negative situations or circumstances in which I was living were simply a reflection of the wrong choices I had made due to my limiting beliefs. Once I had identified and acknowledged the negative paradigms I had adopted, I took pains to imprint the opposite, more desired belief patterns onto my subconscious mind. As outlined in the exercise above, continuous repetition of any new belief is vital in order to negate the old one.

In time, my circumstances and results began to change. I became a more confident person, knowing that I got to choose the manner in which I showed up for life. This said, I also know that nothing is a waste of time; my own experiences have taught me invaluable lessons that have allowed me to grow into the person I am now.

I now hold totally different, more positive views about money and relationships. And although the past was tough, I am happy and grateful for having had the opportunity to mentally grow.

## Katerina

As human beings, you would think that self-awareness would come naturally to us. I mean, who would be expected to be more self-aware of self, than self? But for most people, this isn't how it works. Discovering what is holding you back takes effort because for most of us, we simply don't realize that it's actually our own subconscious beliefs that are at fault.

As a child, I was lucky enough to have been raised with many positive thought anchors. Mine was a happy childhood, and yet, as I grew into adulthood, there was one major belief that held me back: *What will other people think?*

I was raised in a big city but spent much time within a local community. As is evidenced in many communities, people tend to gossip and talk about each other. So, although at home I would hear positive messages from my parents, such as *Dream big,* and *You can be whatever you want to be,* there was a conflicting message from society which was *Don't shine too brightly.* If you were too smart, too happy, too energetic, too positive, too pretty, too eager, *too much,* the people who made up this community would smirk and whisper comments like: *Who does she think she is?*

At home, I was encouraged to be all that I could be, however, when I went into the world, I always felt as though I should downplay my intrinsic qualities. Especially as a teenager, I didn't want to stick out or be different from everyone else. Over time, I allowed this feeling to become dominant, and I started living a limited life out of fear of living a life that might appear too grand. But, holding myself back because of the *What will the neighbors think* and the *I need to fit in* beliefs limited my ability to achieve all that I wanted to achieve. I held myself back from being all that I could be simply because I wanted to fit in.

It wasn't until the age of almost thirty that I developed enough mental maturity to recognize that these beliefs were holding me back. Upon solid self-reflection, however, I came to understand that although on the surface it looked like *they* were holding me back, in fact, *I* was holding myself back. It was my own internalization of these perceived whispers, my insecurities and fears of what it might mean if I dared to be different that held me back. Once I became aware of the fact that it was my own thoughts and beliefs around what I thought others thought of me that was holding me back, everything started to change.

I came to realize that you cannot always control what goes on outside, but you can always control what goes on inside. And when you understand this, you can choose to manage your internal dialogue differently. This is one of the biggest messages we hope to reinforce throughout this book—the fact that as individuals, we have the power to choose our own thoughts and thus, directly and powerfully influence the course of our own lives.

And so, we are here to work with you now, to help guide you to the understanding that you get to choose your own thoughts and to introduce new mental conditioning that will work for you and no longer against you. Danielle and I have written this book so that you don't have to do it alone.

# CONCEPTS TO REMEMBER

*Use this space to highlight your favorite insights from this chapter.*

- 

- 

- 

- 

- 

-

# 2

# Dispelling Limiting Beliefs

**THE SKY IS NOT THE LIMIT; YOUR MIND IS.**

In Chapter 1, we talked about the importance of internal mental programming and how it affects the way we live our lives. We shared that your limiting beliefs are those negative beliefs about yourself that weaken your self-esteem and stand in the way of your real success.

We all have things we tell ourselves in the quiet recesses of our own minds, such as:

- *I am not smart enough.*
- *I am not strong enough.*
- *I am too young.*
- *I am too old.*
- *I am too fat.*
- *I am too thin.*
- *There's no way I'll ever be able to do that.*

Unfortunately, most people's internal conversations dwell within the constructs of limiting dialogue rather than expansive dialogue.

Are you where you really want to be in life? Whether financially, physically, emotionally, spiritually, or romantically, if you are not living life to the fullest in each of these areas, chances are there are deeply ingrained negative belief patterns that are limiting your progress. Unbeknownst to you, underlying negative thinking is prevalent in your subconscious mind. The good news is that these can be changed. We all have the ability to dispel our own limiting beliefs. We have the power to move from a self-limiting mindset to a self-empowered mindset.

Think about it: the thoughts that consume your mind tend to control your life. So, if your mind is consumed with thoughts of *I can't,* then you probably won't. The good thing is the opposite is also true—that if you have thoughts of *I can,* then yes, you most likely will. So, in order to move confidently in the direction of the things you want, you simply need to dispel those limiting beliefs and recognize that you are in control of your own life.

As we will discuss further in the next chapter, awareness is key. To move your life forward, you must identify and become aware of what your limiting beliefs are and then simply make the choice to alter your perceptions of them. It really is that simple.

# **EXERCISE**

One effective way to help shift and alter your perception is to do an exercise known as *projecting*. No matter what age you are now, know that you will always be younger today than you will be tomorrow. If there is a limiting belief holding you back around the subject of age, for example, the first step is to identify it, to become aware of it.

1. Write down your current age.
2. Now, project yourself fifty years into the future.

   - What does your future-self look like?
   - What is your future-self doing?
   - What amazing things has your future-self achieved?
   - Most importantly, what does your fifty-years-in-the-future-self want to say to your current-self?

Chances are your future-self would say encouraging things to your current-self. Things such as:

- *Stand strong.*
- *Think positively.*
- *Take that chance.*
- *You can do it.*

Although we don't normally talk to our current selves like this, imagine looking back at your life fifty years from now. It is almost inevitable that you would think thoughts, such as: *I was young, and capable, and able, and willing—why did I make the mistake of never even trying?*

So, try you must.

Whatever it is that you want to do or achieve in life, be confident in knowing that your fifty-years-in-the-future-self will likely have wanted you to go for it.

    3. Listen to your future-self and work to change your thoughts *now*.

- Change thoughts of *I'm too old now* to *I'm the perfect age.*

- Change thoughts of *It's too late now* to *Now is the perfect time.*

- Change thoughts of *I can't afford that* to *I can afford it if I put my mind to it.*

- Change thoughts of *I am alone* to *My perfect partner is on the way.*

Overcoming limiting self-talk is essential to creating an overall positive mindset. And it is only with an overall positive mindset that we can truly achieve all that we are destined to achieve.

If you have a dream or a passion that you have always wanted to pursue, but you think that the window of opportunity is long gone, project yourself fifty years into the future. Look back at your life and all the many years still left between now and then.

Framing your life from the position of your future-self will help to put things into a different perspective, a perspective that will assist in shining a spotlight on all the many reasons why you should start to chase that dream today and strive to become the most positive and authentic version of you.

Follow your own personal yellow brick road. Start today to dispel your limiting beliefs. Your future-self will thank you.

*May your choice reflect your hopes, not your fears.*
~ Nelson Mandela

# AUTHORS' PERSONAL EXPERIENCES

*Danielle*

I grew up hearing adults in my own family saying that I was ugly and that I was a bad girl. According to them, I was so bad that raising me was like raising a snake. These adults referred to me as a thing, not as a human being.

I remember hearing these things about myself when I was three—much too young to be labeled with such terrible words. I was not mature enough then to analyze and filter what might be true or false about me or my potential, so by default I simply accepted everything as being the absolute truth, with no objections.

As a teenager, my internal dialogue shaped itself in agreement with those beliefs. I used to believe that I could not accomplish big things because I was not intelligent enough. I used to believe that nobody would like me because I was ugly and unpleasant to look at. I used to believe that nothing I ever did was good enough.

Well, that sort of self-talk is absurd and unreasonably cruel, but it's what I believed. At the time, I hadn't understood that those were simply the beliefs of others, and they had no bearing whatsoever on what I could choose to believe about myself. I didn't realize that I had a choice to think differently about myself.

Some years ago, when I started to study the human mind, I decided to become my own test subject, and I applied the principles of replacing negative beliefs about myself with positive ones. I became conscious of changing my own internal dialogue from:

- *I am afraid to I am brave.*
- *I am ugly to I am beautiful.*
- *I am stupid to I am intelligent.*
- *I feel ashamed to I feel confident.*

The more I changed my internal dialogue, the more I came to believe in the power of the thoughts that I wanted to serve me.

In the beginning, I felt like I was trying to fool myself, trying to be something I was not. However, as time went by, I started to notice that my perception about myself was changing. No big change took place at once, but, little by little, I started to experience shifts in my own attitude because of the new way I began to perceive myself and my circumstances.

We are going to more fully address the importance of attitude in a later chapter, but for now, just know that the first step in moving toward the direction of the things you want is to identify and then replace your limiting beliefs. As I did this, my excitement about my potential began to grow, and I recognized more and more the incredible importance of monitoring your own thoughts.

Don't wait any longer to dispel your limiting beliefs. Your future-self will thank you.

## *Katerina*

Limiting beliefs can be tricky to identify because for many of us, we may not have even realized that there is a limiting belief at play. Many of us simply assume that life is the way it is because that's just *how it is*. But, without taking the time to look deeply into your belief patterns and where they come from, you may go through life living with only a fraction of the true spirit, energy, and alertness that you were intended to experience.

While identifying limiting beliefs is hard, dispelling them is even harder. That's because the paradigm often runs deep, due to the many years of seeding. I remember being a twenty-two-year-old, new university graduate and thinking to myself: *I have so much time until I reach the age of thirty.*

Suddenly, I was thirty. And by the time I was in my mid-thirties, I was literally having a panic attack because of all the things I hadn't yet achieved, according to society's checklist:

- I was thirty-four years old and still not married.
- I was thirty-four years old and still not a mother.
- I was thirty-four years old and still living in an apartment building rather than in a house with a white picket fence.
- I was thirty-four years old and still not an A-list television star.

My limiting beliefs started to speak loudly to me, especially the belief that *I'm too old now*. Although, as a child, I had grown up being told I could be or do anything, I had somehow lost that confidence as I got older. By the time I was in my mid-thirties, I had let limiting beliefs, like *You're too old to get married now*, and *It's too late to start a new career* overtake my being and in turn, my well-being.

That is why the exercise we outlined earlier in this chapter is such a powerful one. You owe it to yourself to recognize how truly perfect your current-self is. You will never be younger or more alive than you are right now. Don't let limiting beliefs stand in the way of all the good you are capable of achieving.

For me, I shifted my internal beliefs from:

- *I'm too old now to I am the perfect age.*
- *It's too late now to There is plenty of time.*
- *I can't to Of course, I can.*

I learned to shift my mindset and the perception of my current reality by taking the time to do the internal work. I identified what beliefs I held and put a special spotlight on the ones that I felt were not in my best interest. I then took the time to list new beliefs, which aimed at dispelling the limiting ones. In time, the new beliefs became my default setting. In turn, I became happier, more successful, and wealthier than ever before.

Was it easy? No. It takes time and diligent effort to consciously choose your thoughts. But, it is this conscious effort that has made all the difference.

# CONCEPTS TO REMEMBER

*Use this space to highlight your favorite insights from this chapter.*

- 

- 

- 

- 

- 

-

# 3

# Take 100 Percent Responsibility

**YOU HAVE CREATED YOUR OWN CIRCUMSTANCES, AND ONLY YOU HAVE THE POWER TO CHANGE THEM.**

Every situation you are currently living is simply a reflection of a past decision you have made. If there are aspects of your life that you aren't satisfied with, you must recognize that you had a large part in creating them. If you don't, you'll continue to live in a limiting, victim mentality. As a self-proclaimed victim, life is not easy.

This concept may require a little extra effort to understand, so it is important to review what we previously discussed regarding mental conditioning. Most people are accustomed to blaming their current negative circumstance on others, rarely on themselves. They have false limiting beliefs ingrained deep into their subconscious minds, and because of this, they often take on the role of victim in their own life.

It's common to see teenagers quit school and take the first poorly paying job they stumble upon simply because they need the money. They look for short-term gratification: to buy the trendiest cell phone on the market, the coolest clothes and trinkets, those hot music festival tickets, and so on.

At the time, this feels like the right decision—living in the moment, not thinking about tomorrow. But when adulthood comes around, these same people then find themselves living in a home that they don't own, in an area of the city where they don't feel safe, working a job they don't like, and earning a sub-par salary, which may not even be enough to cover the monthly bills.

These people complain that life is unfair, that they aren't being given a break. They blame the government for their lack and limitation. They blame their family for not providing more opportunity. They blame the system for being unfair. But the reason many of these people blame their circumstances rather than take responsibility for the direction of their own lives is because many times, they don't even realize they have the power to do so.

The universe is absolutely fair and works under precise laws, one of them being the universal Law of Cause and Effect: for every action, there's an equal and opposite reaction. Physics is complex, but for our purposes here we'll sum it up using this simple lifestyle analogy: good choices = good results; bad choices = bad results.

Another commonality that doesn't usually serve people is that the average person tends to raise children to believe that safety comes at the expense of risk-taking. But, the truth is that even if you play it safe and never take a risk, nothing in life is guaranteed.

There's no such thing as luck: the universe is fair and works in an orderly way, giving each and every one of us exactly the same access to thought. And it is thought and thinking that create opportunities. Your mental conditioning makes you think, feel, and act according to your most limiting belief. All the decisions you have made, all the accomplishments you have achieved, all the things you have done or have not done are a result of the beliefs currently held in your subconscious mind.

The quality of your relationships, your health condition, your job, your financial situation, the house you live in, everything, in fact, is a direct result of your mental programming. And it's this mental programming that drives the decisions you make and thus the results you achieve in life. Of course, it is also important to point out that many of the achievements you are proud of are also the result of your mental programming. In this case, they are the result of the positive anchors and beliefs you hold.

And so, it is important to be aware that you are 100 percent responsible for directing the course of your own life. You cannot blame your parents or your employer or your government or society at large for the beliefs that were transferred to you since you now have the power to change those beliefs if you so desire. The good news is that once you make the decision to take responsibility for your own thoughts, belief patterns, feelings, and actions, you regain the power to steer your life in the direction you want it to go. In time, you'll come to see that negative results are nothing more than evidence of past ways of thinking. Change your thoughts, change your results.

> *Your results today are merely the reflection of your subconscious thoughts and beliefs of yesterday.*
> ~ Bob Proctor

It is time to realize that the outer world can only be changed by changing the inner self-dialogue. The first change you need to make is within yourself: the key lies with your own thinking.

*There is only one corner of the universe you can be certain of improving, and this is your own self.*
~ Aldous Huxley

Chapters 1 and 2 are intended to help make you aware of the fact that that many of the perceptions you previously held were due to the thought patterns that you inadvertently absorbed as a child. In this chapter, we bring awareness to the role you played in making the decisions that have shaped your life.

You must reconcile your choices and take 100 percent responsibility for your current results in order to free up room in your mind to build new habits and thought patterns. It is through these more focused and consciously chosen thoughts that you will have the power to create circumstances rather than simply feel at the mercy of them.

People who recognize that certain foods help make their body healthier, but who then go out and eat junk food, shouldn't complain about their ensuing health problems. They have repeatedly made the decision to eat food that is causing their body to malfunction. In the same vein, people who know that certain work environments are stifling and not nourishing, but who decide to stay put anyway, should not blame their employer for their lack of career progression.

There's always a choice, even if at times, the choice may simply consist of recognizing that you have the power to control your own thoughts. Remember the lotus flower: even though its environment is a swamp surrounded by muddy water, the lotus flower grows with such breathtaking beauty that it cannot go unnoticed. You can never blame anyone, any place, or any situation for the life you are living. Good or bad, you created it through your own thoughts and subsequent actions and decisions.

Now that you are aware, understand that all you need to do is make up your mind that you are going to succeed, and you will succeed. Make up your mind to no longer allow anyone to cause you to feel bad about yourself; you will no longer allow them to because you now know that you have the ability to reject any idea that doesn't suit you. Once you decide that you are ultimately the one in control of your own thoughts, you will assume your role as the captain of your own ship. You will start to take back your own power to create the circumstances you want, rather than remain the victim of circumstances supposedly created by others.

*Don't wait for extraordinary opportunities.*
*Seize common occasions and make them great.*
*Weak men wait for opportunities; strong men make them.*
~ Orison Swett Marden

Life is full of opportunities, everywhere, for everyone, all the time. Know that everything you need to succeed in life is already accessible to you through the power of your own thoughts. Make a point from this day forward to focus only on thought patterns that support your growth.

# EXERCISE

1. Make a list, including brief descriptions, of some recent events in which the situation you were in, and the way you chose to deal with it, lead to an unwanted result.

   For example:

   *Yesterday, when I was driving home from work, a driver cut me off. I got angry and started arguing with him in my head. By the time I got home, I had a terrible headache. Because of this headache, I wasn't able to spend quality time with my kids. I felt annoyed and sad; my children were disappointed.*

2. For each event, now rewrite the description, substituting the outcome with one you would have preferred had you consciously chosen to act differently:

   *Yesterday, when I was driving home from work, a driver cut me off. Although I felt he was in the wrong, I simply chose to ignore him and continued my drive home. Perhaps he was just in a hurry. When I got home, my kids warmly received me. We had a wonderful dinner, and then I spent time playing with my kids. I feel so appreciative of my ability to spend quality time with the people I love.*

Create the habit of thinking before reacting and you will begin to see that you truly have the power to mold circumstances to the manner of your choosing.

> *I am the master of my fate, I am the captain of my soul.*
> Excerpt from the poem "Invictus"
> by William Ernest Henley

# AUTHORS' PERSONAL EXPERIENCES

*Danielle*

It's not difficult to imagine that before I was exposed to the concepts we share in this book, I was drowning in negative self-perception. As a result, my life was simply ordinary, average, mediocre, and I blamed everything and everyone else for the state of my circumstances. I never took responsibility for them.

There was not one area of life where I felt I was winning, but I attributed this lack of success to the way I was raised. I attributed it also to my own lack of intelligence, to the lack of conducive economic conditions, to the lack of societal opportunity, and so on and so on.

Only when I started to pay attention to the quality of the decisions I had been making did I realize that everything I was experiencing was the result of my own choices.

When asked in job interviews how much I would like to earn, because of my lack of confidence, I used to answer that the minimum salary was okay. What kind of salary do you think they would pay me after that? Well, my decision, my result, my responsibility.

When at work, I used to view people who had university degrees as people to be revered, while I was someone who should feel ashamed, since I didn't have one. I used to underestimate my intelligence in comparison to theirs thinking that since they held a degree, they must be more intelligent than I. This way of thinking and feeling about myself used to paralyze any intentions on my part to try to do better.

I used to think: *Well, I am a creative person, but the ideas I have are ideas of someone who lacks a degree, so why would anyone pay attention?* I would choose to keep my head down rather than speak up. What I didn't realize at the time was that not doing something was also a type of decision, and that this kind of behavior was keeping me stuck.

When I interacted with people I knew weren't good company, I pitied myself. In the end, I used to drown in a sea of disappointment. What I know now is that I had chosen not to listen to what my intuition was trying to tell me. It knew that putting energy into those types of relationships was contrary to what I needed. But I chose to ignore it because my limiting thought patterns were too pervasive. In the end, I had no choice but to consciously work at changing my beliefs. And I am so glad that I did!

Take 100 percent responsibility for the choices you make, for if you do, you will hone your ability to cultivate awareness, and that is when big changes start to take place.

## Katerina

In the early part of my career, I was making great money for my age. After a few years, I decided to take some time off to travel. The economy changed for the worse, and my assets started to diminish. My stock options collapsed, my real estate investments lost significant value, my savings had been spent having fun in Europe, and suddenly I found myself in a negative monetary situation. I was in debt—something I had never before experienced.

I complained that the economy was at fault, but you see, I was not taking 100 percent responsibility for my financial situation. I had made my money. But then, I had decided to spend my money. Yes, there were real fluctuations that happened with the economy, but the down turn I experienced had to do not only with those market fluctuations but with my inability to properly manage my own assets.

The mistake I started making was placing the blame on everyone but myself for the financial conditions I found myself in. Only when I became real, raw, and honest with myself did the behavior, and my results, change.

Maturity comes when you stop making excuses and start making change. So, take 100 percent responsibility for your life. Because you are indeed the one in charge.

# CONCEPTS TO REMEMBER

*Use this space to highlight your favorite insights from this chapter:*

- 

- 

- 

- 

- 

-

# 4

# Your Life's Purpose

**DO WHAT MAKES YOU FEEL ALIVE.**

Remember when you were young, and you used to dream of all the things you wanted to be when you grew up?

You may have dreamt of becoming an astronaut, a scientist, a doctor, or a firefighter. Perhaps you wanted to be an author, a movie star, or the country's leader. The list of choices was infinite.

As a child, you simply allowed yourself to dream, without worrying about the *how*. You didn't dwell on all the things that could possibly hinder your path. You simply felt enthusiasm for all the possibilities, and you let your imagination run wild.

How did you feel?

Invincible? Fearless? Excited?

But, as you got older, perhaps the adults who loved you thought it wise to shield you from the risk and frustration of failed dreams. Perhaps they hadn't achieved their childhood dreams, and because of this, they measured your future success probability through the parameters and perceptions of their own limited experiences.

As you grew older, perhaps they started to caution you against the pursuit of those dreams. A child who dreamt of becoming a professional painter might have been told that it was difficult to make a solid living as a painter. Perhaps his parents suggested that he become a lawyer instead, since *lawyers make good money*. A child who had always dreamt of being in the movies was perhaps told by the people she loved that she could never make it because *the only people who made it in Hollywood were those who already had strong, established connections*. Perhaps it was implied that she would be better off studying to become an engineer—now that's a real career.

Little by little, children are often discouraged from daydreaming and encouraged instead to play it safe. From the parent's perspective, this is the right thing to do. But as a result, children often end up pursuing a career that has nothing to do with their true passion.

The biggest mistake we see people make is that of losing their integrity to self, due to their unwillingness to chase their dreams and pursue their passions. People feel the pressure to play it safe. They conform to safer expectations by resigning themselves to a less than fulfilling career. In turn, they are not happy. Because of the drive to conform, they end up living a life much less rich than the one they were designed to be living. They become a shadow of the living being that they were born to be.

We are spiritual beings, and the nature of spirit is toward continual expansion. When we fail to explore all that we are truly capable of exploring, we often feel incredible amounts of frustration over those unexplored expansion possibilities. Imagine buying a Ferrari and trying to force it onto off-road paths. It simply hasn't been designed for that kind of terrain. The Ferrari doesn't have feelings, but if it were a living creature, do you think it would feel as though it was performing at its fullest potential while on the wrong path? Probably not.

Can you relate this example to your own experience? Can you truly say that you have allowed yourself to explore the ultimate path, the one that can provide you with access to your greatest achievement potential?

When we were young, we used our imagination frequently, until the mental lids and the invisible limits that conditioned us to live at lower standards began to shackle us.

How many people do you know who appear successful on paper but who are not at all happy in their careers? So many people struggle to find joy because they don't feel fulfilled in their careers. This is a sign: life is showing them that they are off course. People in these situations are constantly thinking about retirement, whereas the people who love their work because it is their passion don't consider it work at all—they want to keep *working* until the end of their days.

Why are so many people living someone else's dream? Think of the son who had incredible skills in artistry and craftsmanship, but who became an accountant because his father wanted him to become an accountant. Perhaps he achieved professional success but did he achieve contentment? Think of the girl who loved to give her friends makeovers and did a phenomenal job at it. But instead of pursuing a career as an aesthetician, she bent to the pressures of society and conceded to an office job. She ended up behind a desk, filing paper and spending energy in a way that was completely misaligned with her true passion and innate gifts.

Are you content? The question you need to ask yourself is this: *Am I getting up every day and working on what I'm working on because of the passion I have for it, or am I working simply for the money and the security?* Money is great, but to what extent are you denying yourself the gift of living into your highest potential by denying yourself the opportunity to pursue your dreams?

When people don't create from a place of soulful alignment, they disintegrate. Why? Because they are behaving contrary to their intrinsic human nature. Because of this misalignment, many people develop disease, depression, or other types of physical or spiritual pain. They are not living the life they are designed to live.

If you are in a profession which you adore, congratulations!

A well-defined purpose gives meaning to life: it's the *why* you go to bed full of gratitude and get up excited for the day to come. When you are passionate about your work, you derive energy from it, similar to that of an extra power source. It makes you feel complete because you are expressing yourself entirely, with no reservations. This way, you can contribute and add value to the world. When you work in alignment with your true mission, everyone benefits from the quality of service you render and everyone wins.

Full expansion and expression are possible for each of us, but only by doing what you truly love will you be able to explore your true creative potential.

If you haven't yet figured out your purpose, don't despair. Simply start by identifying things you don't like doing. This will help you to narrow in on what it is that you do like to do. By figuring out what you don't like doing, you identify what doesn't feel right. When something doesn't feel right to you, it means that it's not in alignment with your soul. When something doesn't feel right, recognize that the discomfort you feel is there to highlight that more is available to you.

Even if you don't yet know what your life's purpose is, you can start homing in by identifying your strengths. Things that come naturally to you are the things you should pay attention to. If you have good communication skills, work on developing them further. If you are good at writing, write more often and about topics you love. If you are a good athlete, develop that unique skill. You don't have to work on your weaknesses. Focus on your talents and innate skills. Listen carefully to your inner voice; it will lead you to your infinite power. It will connect you with Source, with your true self.

Dare to dream again. Take time to imagine all the possibilities. The time is now to respect yourself enough to honor what is truly in your soul. What would you do if you knew that there was no chance of failing; that success was guaranteed? What mark do you want to leave on humanity?

# **EXERCISE**

This exercise is intended to help you discern your life's purpose.

1. Think of a recent experience you enjoyed and describe it. For example:

   *I have been chosen to write and share children's stories at my daughter's school.*

2. Write down the emotions you felt during this experience.

   *At first, I was a little scared because I haven't written in a long time. But the more I wrote, the more inspired I felt. By the end of the hour, I felt amazing.*

3. What skills did you exhibit during this experience?

   *Creative writing, language skills, storytelling abilities, imaginative thought creation.*

4. Identify and list the intrinsic qualities you exhibited.

   *Creativity, passion, imagination. I recognize that I am good at sharing stories.*

5. Which part of the process did you most enjoy?

   *The writing*

6. How can you honor and celebrate this passion more fully today?

   *I can write books aimed at helping children discover the beauty of the written word. I can write poetry or inspirational text. I can work with students to help cultivate their love of writing.*

The path to your purpose can be sought by taking the time to analyze which tasks you perform that make you feel alive. Discovering your purpose can be likened to falling in love. Nobody else can tell you when you are in love; you simply know it. So, don't be afraid to seek out and then fall madly in love with your purpose and passions.

But remember, finding your purpose is different than goal setting. An example of a goal might be buying a new car, a new house, or taking a vacation. Goals are accomplishments, but purpose validates your life as an individualized expression of the universe's energetic intent for continued creation.

First, seek to *be*, and all the rest will come to you.

By spending more time doing what you were inherently designed to do, you align your self with your purpose—you tune in to the why in why you are here. And you can positively affect other people's lives. We are all connected. When you move in accordance with your true mission, you increase the probability of positively impacting others. We are all here to help create the best life we can.

You are here to make a difference in other people's lives. And the more you share of yourself, the more fulfillment you gain from life and from others. Discover your purpose, your worthy ideal, your mission, and you'll hold the treasure map to happiness and fulfillment in your hands.

*When the personality comes fully to serve the energy of its soul, that is authentic empowerment.*
~ Gary Zukav

# AUTHORS' PERSONAL EXPERIENCES

*Danielle*

The way I stumbled upon my life's purpose is funny because it happened absolutely unexpectedly.

The marketing company I was working for at the time sent me to a networking, communication, and personal branding conference. By the way, I wasn't even supposed to go, but things happened, and there I was.

The first two speakers presented. I was enjoying my time there, but nothing really seemed special until the last speaker, Silvana Lages, took the stage. She was so magnetic. She had such a powerful presence and such an honest way of delivering her message that in that very moment, it was if I had been struck by lightning. I said to myself: *This is it. This is what I want to do for the rest of my life. I want to be a transformational speaker and motivator.* And angels started to sing—okay, just kidding. But I felt like heaven had opened its golden gates for me to walk through, red carpet laid out and all.

I have always been passionate about sharing knowledge and information that I knew would be of value to others. Yet, until that moment I had never realized that I could do a phenomenal job if I started to pursue this work as my purpose. I love to help people, to empower them, to share valuable information, to add value to the world. Why had I never before thought about living my life doing this every day?

I am happy and grateful that I have been blessed in discovering my true passion and in having the opportunity to live its full expression. It is incomparable, this feeling of fulfillment and gratitude that started to hold a place in my heart when I decided to pursue my *mission*, to work on purpose. Now, I truly understand the good that I can do for others because I am living my truth.

Give it a try. We are here to serve.

## *Katerina*

Unlike Danielle, I always knew what I wanted to be when I grew up. My passion, my dream, my destiny was to become a television host and share news and information with the world. Not an actress. Trust me when I say I cannot act, but I can host. I knew this when I was a little girl. Give me a microphone and watch me shine. Put a person in the seat next to me and allow me to interview them all day, every day. That is my passion and it always has been.

But I didn't really start pursuing my dream of building a career in television until the age of almost forty. Why? Because I allowed other people's opinions, preferences, and ideas of how I should live my life influence my early decisions. Instead of listening to my spiritual guidance system, I instead listened to what society thought I should be and do.

You see, although I always knew I wanted to be in television and media, I studied finance in university instead, because that was the safer, more logical choice. I went to school for four years and graduated with a degree in business. And then, I even went on to study an even more advanced discipline of finance. Upon graduation, I proceeded to work in the corporate sector. But I wasn't fulfilled. That's when I knew it was time to start listening to my own guidance system, to that little voice within.

At the time, I had a job that rewarded me with a great salary, good benefits, an ego-satisfying job title, and a corner office. But, I was miserable. Why? Because I wasn't living my passion. I wasn't living my dream. I wasn't optimizing the natural talents I had been given—public speaking, onstage presence, articulation in communication, and quick-wittedness on my feet.

Instead of listening to my heart and taking a chance on myself, I had played it safe. And, by doing so, I found myself in a place where I did not feel alive. And the whole point of being alive is to *feel* alive—and happy, and joyous, and excited, and creative, and optimistic, and content. If you are not feeling that way, then something is not right. We come into this world to enjoy the fullest experience of life. But too many of us do not.

Do you feel as alive as you know, deep down, you should?

Please take the time now, while you are working through this book, to be honest with yourself about your current situation. Does what you are currently doing truly make your heart sing? Perhaps you are working as a teacher, but you would prefer to be a landscaper because you love nature. Or, perhaps you drive a truck, but have always dreamt of being a professional painter. Or perhaps you build homes, but you have always had an aptitude for numbers and would like to go back to school and study accounting.

Listen to your heart.

You are equipped with intrinsic gifts for a reason. Only when we truly honor those gifts, can we tap into the truest version of ourselves and offer our greatness to the world. When we honor what really makes us feel alive, we have the power to impact the world.

# CONCEPTS TO REMEMBER

*Use this space to highlight your favorite insights from this chapter:*

- 

- 

- 

- 

- 

- 

-

# 5

# Build Your Vision

**LET YOUR IMAGINATION GUIDE THE WAY.**

If you haven't figured out what your purpose is yet, don't worry. Let's start with keeping calm and recognizing that taking time for self on a daily basis will help you still your mind and gain more clarity. We recommend allocating ten to twenty minutes per day for relaxation. Meditate, take a walk in nature, sit quietly and listen to music, take a bath. Whatever your method of choice, take some time for self.

Then, while in a relaxed state of mind, concentrate your thoughts on seeking your purpose. Try and really tune in to the core of *you* by being still and simply listening for guidance from Source.

Don't stress out if you don't discover your purpose in a day, or a week, or a month, or even longer. Remain disciplined and take the time daily to still your mind, trusting that you will hear the whispers you need to hear in order to add clarity to your question. Once you have identified more clearly what your purpose might be, it's then time to build your vision—the way you want to live because you are working on purpose—an inspiring vision that will keep you excited and energized about the life you are leading.

All of us are equipped with one of the most marvelous intellectual faculties: the imagination. Effective use of the imagination ensures we will always have access to the resources we need by tapping into the power of our own thoughts. Dig deep into your soul and bring to the surface the desires you hold. Ask yourself: *What gets my blood pumping? What causes my heart to beat stronger? What makes me excited and enthusiastic?*

Free your imagination. Let it fly. See yourself doing what you love, living the life of your dreams, spending more quality time with your loved ones, traveling the world, interacting with rich and abundant friends. And then, feel all the emotions associated with those visions: feel the love, the fulfillment, the passion, the abundance, the gratitude, the grace, the joy.

One tool that helps the subconscious mind hold the vision is the construction of a vision board. Create a vision board and place it where you can see it, dedicating time both morning and night to looking at it and feeling into it. Continuous repetition of the viewing of the images on the board will rewire your brain in a way that creates cells of recognition for the things you desire. By viewing these images daily, their essence gets embedded in your emotional mind.

Not quite sure how to build a vision board? Don't worry, it's very easy. First, identify and imagine the things you want to manifest in your life: the car you want to have, your dream home, the places you want to travel to, the lifestyle you want to live. Next, using magazine photos or images you print off the internet, collect shots of the things that represent what you want and then glue or tape them onto a flat board. This then becomes your vision board.

By creating a vision board, you are planting in your subconscious mind imaginative images of the ideal life you want to create. By communicating these images—and more importantly, the emotions behind them—to your deepest self, you will begin to accelerate your being's ability to manifest those desires into physical form. Once you have identified the things that you want, hold these powerful and inspiring images in your mind during your ten to twenty minutes of relaxation. Anything that you can see in your mind's eye can, in fact, materialize in the physical world.

In addition to creating a vision board, journaling is also a powerful way to cement your dreams and desires deeply in your subconscious mind. Go ahead and write down your vision in the present tense. The subconscious mind has no ability to differentiate between what's real and what is not. Whatever you feel, it will take as truth. Describe every detail of the things you want: the colors, the smells, the textures, the sounds, the tastes, and most importantly, the feelings that those things bring up in you. Paint your vision with words.

To get you started, here is a short example of how you can begin journaling your vision:

> *I am so happy and grateful now that I am living the life of my dreams.*
>
> *I am a (name what you do), recognized worldwide and respected. The service that I render helps the world be a better place for all.*
>
> *I live in the home of my dreams, with the most incredible view of the sea. I spend my days smelling the sea salt, hearing the crashing of the waves on the shore, feeling the warm and gentle breeze that comes to fill my soul with life.*
>
> *My family is living in so much happiness and abundance, they spread to the universe all the wonderful energy they have within them. Everybody who comes into contact with us leaves with the impression of*

*increasing and a renewed sense of purpose for themselves and their mission.*

*I have meaningful friendships and kind friends who bring out the very best in me, as I bring out the very best in them. I love to see them accomplishing their dreams.*

*The more connected I become with my own purpose and soul's calling, the more I see evidence of all the miracles taking place in my life. This allows me to value and give back to other people, leading me further into the living of a life that is rich with grace and gratitude.*

Build up what we call *future memories* and live into them. Feel inspired by them and know, in your heart, that all of them are available to you.

The imagination is a mental faculty that is incredibly powerful. So, go ahead, build your vision with exacting detail. Allow yourself to get emotionally involved with it. Look at your vision board daily. If journaling, write down and then read your vision out loud. Do this for ninety days and get ready to see your life transform.

Anything you see that has ever been created by human beings was created twice: first as a thought in the mind of a person, and second as materialized physical form.

> *I dream my painting, and then I paint my dream.*
> ~ Vincent Van Gogh

Be consistent and don't allow your old paradigm to distract you. If you really want to change, you must to be willing to do this mental work with discipline and dedication. So, make it your new habit and commit to doing these daily practices. If you do, you will soon begin to see evidence of your desires manifested in your physical reality.

> *Imagination is everything. It is the preview of life's coming attractions.*
> ~ Popular saying

# AUTHORS' PERSONAL EXPERIENCES

*Danielle*

In my opinion, I believe that everyone visualizes; however, many don't do it consciously. They don't realize that the images they hold in the quiet of their minds deeply affect the creative process, and in turn, affect the way their lives unfold. People fantasize about things they wish they had. Like a sort of parallel reality, they live an imaginary life, if only in their thoughts. The thing is, if the images they see are limiting, evidence of limitation will appear in their present reality without them realizing it. Other times the images they see are positive ones, but the strength behind the vision is compromised because they don't believe they are really capable of achieving what they dream of.

I have always had a very active imagination. Long before I was formally exposed to the idea of conscious visioning techniques, I had played with various ideas of what I would want my life to look like. I was imagining my ideal life. In bed, before I would fall asleep, I would imagine the things I wanted. It felt like I was watching a movie, and that I was the main star. In the depths of my imagination, I was living my ideal life. The astonishing part of this is that a lot of what I had in my imagination actually came to pass several years later.

As a child, one of my fantasies was to marry a man named Richard. I simply don't know why, but I loved this name. I thought that it was the most beautiful male name in the world. It was many years later before I realized that my husband's name, Ricardo, is the Portuguese version of the name Richard!

Another thing I used to fantasize about was living abroad. And here I am today, living in Portugal rather than in my native Brazil.

I also used to envision myself as a writer, seeing myself spending nights writing my books. Although I am not a full-blown professional writer by trade, I did co-author this book, one which I feel is simply the first of many. I so thoroughly enjoyed writing this book—filling it with all my love and good energy in order to touch as many lives as I could with the amazing messages that are shared throughout its pages. These messages have shaped and continue to shape my life in the most positive of ways.

When I became formally aware of the visualization technique and its power to shape reality, I became conscious of not allowing my own limiting beliefs to enter the picture. I no longer allow things like doubt, fear, or uncertainty to dictate what I imagine because I realize that the power of visualization comes from being crystal clear on the things I desire, not on the things that I don't. In the past, although I used to envision big things in my life, I did so from a place of mild amusement and self-entertainment because many times, I still felt my dreams were unavailable.

But now, I do it differently. Now, I make sure to infuse every image with affirmative energy and a *yes I can* attitude. Today, I know that anything I envision is available to me. As long as I keep the images clear and backed with the right energy, I know that it is only a matter of time before the things I see in my mind's eye become evident in my physical reality.

Even after all the incredible amount of success I've had over the years, I continue with the upkeep of my vision board. In fact, one whole wall in my living room is dedicated to showcasing images of all the things I want to accomplish, do, and have in my life. The images are compiled in the form of a collage and include photos of places I want to visit, things I want to purchase, and even of people I admire and want to emulate. Even if something feels out of reach, I don't shy away from thinking big.

I place the images there, front and center in my home, so that I can see them often. Seeing them often and already evident in my personal space—even if only in 2D picture format—reminds me that anything is possible for those who believe. Seeing those images daily allows me to become emotionally attached to the desire, and this, in turn, motivates me to strive even harder to see them become a reality. I spend several minutes a day taking time to dwell in the feeling that the images create inside me. Sometimes I'll spend time looking into the eyes of the personalities' photos. I spend time looking at their eyes, connecting myself with them, tuning in to them, their personalities, their wisdom, their success. I spend time feeling the essence of them. This practice is powerful, and it is something I love doing.

Our imagination has the power to unfold a world of unlimited possibilities. Imagination is the starting point of all of humanity's creations. Dream often. Dream big. Dream without limits. Do away with voices of past limitation. Recognize that they don't serve you—shut them down—and simply imagine, without restriction, the life you truly want. Hold that vision and know that you have the ability to accomplish it all.

*Logic will get you from A to B. Imagination will take you everywhere.*
~ Attributed to Albert Einstein

## *Katerina*

*Build your Vision.* As the title of this chapter instructs, taking the time to build a vision for your life is incredibly important. In its simplicity, however, many people overlook the power that visioning holds. A clear vision helps you pursue dreams. Holding an idea of the future, not only as a strong wish but as an unwavering belief, can be absolutely instrumental in propelling you forward toward all the success you desire.

As a little girl, I used to *see* myself on television. I would prance around the house using a hair brush as a microphone, pretending to interview my dolls and anyone who would come to visit for dinner on a Sunday night. As a teenager, that vision expanded to seeing myself living in Hollywood. Thirty years later, that dream became a reality. That fact struck me as I was driving my Mercedes down Rodeo Drive in Beverly Hills one spring day a few years back. I had made it happen!

Sometimes the things you want can manifest quickly. I've had things I envision show up in my life experience within twenty-four hours of my having seen and felt it in my imagination. Other times, as with the example above, they can take years. But if you stick to the vision and hold a true knowing deep within your heart, all your dreams and desires will come to pass, even if it takes a lifetime.

Through the ages, great men and women of vision have shaped the world. One such man was Steve Jobs. Steve Jobs was a hell of a visionary. The founder of Apple wasn't just years ahead of his time. He was decades ahead. In

1983, Steve gave a speech at the International Design Conference in Aspen. In it, he offered incredible insight into how he viewed the future, even going so far as to foreshadow the creation of the iPad. Fast-forward years later and on April 3, 2010, the first iPad was released.

Will your dreams be easy to achieve? Perhaps they will; perhaps they won't. But achieve them you will, so long as you control your thoughts, set your intentions, monitor the emotional frequency of your feelings, and most importantly, stay true to your vision.

# CONCEPTS TO REMEMBER

*Use this space to highlight your favorite insights from this chapter:*

- 

- 

- 

- 

- 

-

# 6

# The Law of Vibration

## WHAT YOU BROADCAST TO THE UNIVERSE IS WHAT IS REFLECTED BACK TO YOU.

In order to manifest the things you want in life, you must understand that the universal force field of creation responds to feelings, emotions, and intentions. Projecting these sends out a vibration. This vibration is then picked up by whatever happens to be vibrating at that same frequency and that person/opportunity/experience then enters your life's experience. This is one of the universal laws: the Law of Vibration.

Everything in this universe is made up of energy. Energy vibrates at different rates of frequency. Matter that appears solid is not actually solid. Put any object under a microscope and you will find in it all matter, tiny particles known as *atoms*. In the *nucleus*, or center of each atom, are *neutrons* and *protons,* and surrounding these are particles known as *electrons.* From the most ethereal gas to the most apparently solid matter, everything is made up of energy. It is simply the rate at which that matter vibrates that determines its shape.

Everything in nature is made up of atoms, which behave both as particles and as waves at the same time. In physics, a wave is an oscillation accompanied by a transfer of energy without the transportation of mass. Well-known examples are electromagnetic waves, such as radio waves, microwaves, infrared radiation, visible light, ultraviolet radiation, x-rays, and gamma rays. It is important to remember that waves are coders and carriers of information.[2]

So, a wave represents movement; it is energy which carries information. Every wave has its own rate of vibration.

In the universe, everything has its rate of vibration or frequency, and between those frequencies, there's no starting point and no endpoint. Thus, because we are all made up of energy, we are all connected. Human beings, however, have the mental capacity to control this energy by thinking thoughts that have the power to determine levels of vibration and frequency.

Even though, at this very moment, you may be sitting in a silent room, we can guarantee there is music available in

---

[2]  wikipedia.org/wiki/Wave

that room, right now. It is music that is being broadcast from different points around the world. If you use a radio to tune in to the frequency of a particular broadcast, it will receive the information that is being transmitted in the form of electromagnetic signals, signals which travel through waves, decoding the broadcast and transforming it into sound waves. Those waves have a frequency, and with the aid of the radio, human ears can interpret them. The ears then convert the sound waves into electrical impulses that are then interpreted by the brain, and it is then, and only then, that you will be able to hear the music which is playing in the room.

In a similar manner, you have energy emanating in and out of your body; the higher the energetic frequency, the more power it has. Like a radio, your brain is a switching station. The cells in your brain produce electromagnetic signals, which allow the molecules in your body to communicate with each other. When you think, you activate those brain cells, which in turn emit recognizable and measurable electromagnetic pulses.

Just like the music signals that are broadcast by the radio stations, your thoughts are quantum waves which are broadcast by you to the universe. They are everywhere. They are energy and, as waves, they carry information. Thoughts can have different frequencies, and because of this, they can be picked up by the minds of those who are resonating at that same frequency.

Thoughts control your emotions, and your emotions control the vibration you are in. If you think positive thoughts, you will feel good, and this means you are operating at a higher vibrational frequency. If you think negative thoughts, you will start feeling down, and this means you are operating at a lower vibrational frequency. In turn, this means that whatever is also operating at that lower frequency will be attracted to you.

The Law of Vibration is always working, whether you are aware of it or not. So, the goal is to strive to maintain positive thoughts which will keep you feeling emotionally well, in order to maintain the higher frequency.

But why would you want to move to a higher vibrational state? As mentioned, we all vibrate energetically at a particular frequency. Higher vibrational frequencies are made up of lighter energy, so the higher your frequency, the lighter you feel, emotionally, mentally, and even physically. You tend to have little or no discomfort in your body, and you experience more clarity in your thoughts and generally more tranquility, joy, and love in your life.

In contrast, lower vibrational states result in denser energy. Your mood and countenance will be darker, and you may experience mental confusion and negative emotions. You are also more likely to experience physical discomfort in your body. Overall, your life takes on a more negative quality, and challenges will seem more pervasive.

The good thing is that all people have been equipped with the ability to feel. So, what we call *feelings* are nothing more than the conscious way to recognize the frequencies we are in. When we talk about the thoughts that attract things to you, we are not talking about the rational thoughts, we are talking about the ones floating under the surface, the thoughts that you *feel*.

In other words, the underlying feeling generated by unconscious processing dictates what you attract. If you believe you are poor, you feel poor. And, because you feel poor, you become poor. In the same way, if you believe you are prosperous it is because you feel prosperous. And ninety-nine times out of a hundred, you will indeed be prosperous.

Your feelings reflect your vibration. A positive vibrational frequency has you feeling good, and you then go out and act based on your good feelings. If you are in a low vibrational frequency, you feel down, and you take actions based on those negative feelings.

As we discussed before, every action you take creates an outcome:

Negative thoughts → Decrease your vibration → Cause you to feel down → Make you take negative actions = Create negative results

Positive thoughts → Increase your vibration → Cause you to feel good → Make you take positive actions = Create positive results

That is how things work on a micro level. Now, let's move from the micro world to the macro world to better understand how you attract things, people, and situations into your life. Even if you are not aware of it, you feel comfortable with whatever is in resonance with your vibration. You prefer to hang around people who like the same things you like. If you like heavy metal music, your tendency is to seek out people who have that same preference in music versus people who don't. We choose to work with people we feel good around, many times because they are vibrating at a similar frequency.

If you are not someone who easily embraces risk, this is likely because you are resistant to moving outside of your comfort zone. When new challenges show up, your preference is most likely to stick with the familiar rather than dive into the unknown. You want to stay within the comforts of your default frequency.

Do you tend to be the type of person who frequents places that feel comfortable to you? If you feel at ease going to fancy restaurants, chances are you will typically choose fancy restaurants to dine in. Whereas if you feel more comfortable in pubs, you'll feel a little out of sorts at the fancy place. You see, you constantly attract things to you, and the ones that resonate most will stick. Whether you realize it or not, you naturally push away whatever is not in harmony with your underlying frequency and vibration.

It's important that you truly understand that you don't attract what you wish for, *you attract who you are.*

When you set an intention, whether consciously or unconsciously, you are directly communicating your wants (or un-wants) to the universe, and the universe will always send a match back to you. Therefore, in order to acquire the things you want, rather than the things you don't want, you must tune your thoughts—and thus your subconscious mind—to the frequency of that which you really want. You must desire it and keep your thoughts uplifted so you can feel positive and motivated in your quest to move toward it.

Direct your thinking toward the experiences you wish to have. Do this with focus and a feeling of expectancy, then notice the many opportunities that show up for you. Have the faith that what you want is already yours and leave the *how* to the universe.

> *You don't get what you wish for.*
> *You don't get what you hope for.*
> *You get what you believe.*
> ~ Oprah Winfrey

Be aware that simply thinking positive thoughts, however, is not enough. Positive thinking alone won't manifest what you desire. You could say *I would love to be rich* but if deep down you feel poor, there will be a conflict between what you think and what you feel, and when this is the case, *what you feel will always win.*

Therefore, you must attempt to truly believe what you say to yourself. You must feel it in your heart. You must believe that the good you desire is already yours, ready to be manifested in your life as you go along in your journey, and then take the action steps in your daily life to help accelerate its reality. This is the way you truly tune in to the frequency of the good you desire. There must be an alignment between rational thought and subconscious belief. This is why the power of repetition is so important. You must repeat a thought over and over again until you truly believe it.

How many people do you know who claim to think positively, but when you look at their results, all you see is a big mess of unfortunate events and poor accomplishments? People's results are the perfect indicator of what is really going on with their subconscious thinking. They may claim that they think positively, but deep inside, they don't believe their own words.

*He thinks in secret and it comes to pass.*
*Environment is but his looking glass.*

~ James Allen

Your deepest beliefs and the emotions held by them are what help tune your own personal frequency, and it is that frequency that then goes out to the word. It is that frequency that then resonates with other like-frequencies and attracts things, people, and opportunities vibrating at that same frequency back to you.

Perhaps you want to manifest more wealth in your life, but you don't feel wealthy today. You might verbally state: *I am wealthy,* but inside you hear that internal voice telling you that *this is ridiculous, you are not wealthy, and you know it. Who are you trying to fool?*

Instead of making claims that in the moment may feel hard to believe, use softer, more general language to get you started. A suggestion would be to start saying instead: *I am prosperous in every area of my life. Every day, I become even more prosperous, and I am constantly attracting to me everything and everyone who adds prosperity and wealth to my life.*

Do you feel the difference? With the second, more general statement, you are not telling yourself any blatant falsehoods. Your mind doesn't need to reject the statement because the statement is much more general than the first statement of *I am wealthy*. By using general language, you keep your thoughts and feelings about wealth and prosperity uplifted which then helps to move you to a more positive and lively vibration. Choosing general statements will help you keep a positive attitude as you move toward all that you want.

By choosing more general statements for your affirmations, you eliminate any internal conflict while training your mind to focus on the positive. This assures you are constantly in expectancy of the good you wish to see and feel.

In addition to positive general affirmations, a second way to tune your frequency toward the abundant life you have always dreamt of is to start a gratitude practice. Gratitude instantly shifts your frequency to a higher level, which will immediately start to move you toward the exceptional things you want to attract in to your life.

Even if you are experiencing difficult moments right now, there are certainly things in your life that you can find to be grateful for. For instance, if you are unemployed and stressed about finding another job, remind yourself that this particular instant doesn't define who you are as a person; this is simply a moment in your life, one from which you can learn and grow. Be grateful for the experience to assess choices you may have had the opportunity to assess.

Take this seemingly negative time as an opportunity to feel deeply into self to identify what you do want. Be grateful for the strength and grace you are exhibiting as you move through the current experience.

Use this time to view the situation from different angles. Perhaps because of the comfort and security of your previous job, you hadn't considered the possibility of moving out of your comfort zone. This might be a great time to do some research into what it would take to start your own company, to become an entrepreneur and master of your own empire. How many people do you see who, after many years of dedication to a company, get laid off? Some decide to start their own business. And this new business helps to lead them to succeed beyond their wildest dreams. Wouldn't you agree that the loss of their job was actually a blessing in disguise?

You may be experiencing hardship right now but have faith in knowing that the hardship is simply preparing you for something greater. It is strengthening you. It is teaching you how to develop skills and talents that you would never otherwise have known you had.

A daily gratitude practice helps to hone your mind toward seeing the good in things; if you missed your bus to work and have to walk, realize that that is an opportunity to appreciate the flowers along the way, to be at one with nature, to take a moment to have a conversation with yourself, to tune in to your feelings, and start to consciously become alert to your own vibrational state.

Learn to focus your attention on identifying the good in any particular situation, irrespective of how challenging that situation may appear to be on the surface.

Things to feel grateful for may include:

- Your good health
- Family who love you unconditionally
- Friends whom you can turn to for support
- The intelligence you are gifted with
- Your very own resilience in the moment

A mother we know lost her only daughter. Even though it was a horrific and life-changing time for her, she decided that her daughter's life should be celebrated, not mourned. Instead of thinking her own life had ended the moment her daughter had died and forever mourning her painful loss, she chose instead to be thankful for the time they had together.

She chose to feel thankful for having had her daughter bless her life for those short years, thankful for having had the opportunity to live and really understand unconditional love, thankful for having felt the deep love of a child. Most importantly, she chose to be grateful for the gift of having loved so deeply. Even amidst tragedy beyond comprehension, this woman chose to be grateful for the time they shared and continues to this day to celebrate life.

Everyone deals with deeply difficult moments in different ways, but as this mother proved, if you can cultivate gratitude and choose to see the positive in any situation, life will become remarkably beautiful.

If you seek the negative, you will find it. If you seek the positive, you will find it. Since this is the case, and you have the power to choose how you feel in any given moment, why choose anything less than the best? Even if you need to dig deep, know that in any situation, under any circumstance, there is always something to be grateful for.

Train yourself to think positive thoughts and allow yourself to become deeply emotionally involved with them in order to really feel the positivity in the cells of your being. Know that if you do, you will be emanating a strong vibration to the universe, a high frequency, which will then reciprocate by sending high frequency experiences, people and opportunities into your reality.

# **EXERCISE**

1. Start a gratitude journal. Daily—preferably in the morning, so you can start up your days with uplifted thoughts and emotions—allocate time to identifying and listing ten things you are grateful for.

2. Once down on paper, take a few minutes to read each point, feeling the intensity of the gratitude behind the sentiment. Emotion is key.

3. Take the time to do this for ninety days. Before you know it, and when you least expect it, you will realize that gratitude has become your natural state, and you will have successfully shifted your internal vibration to that coveted higher frequency.

The Law of Vibration is at play, all the time, whether you are aware of it or not. Tune to a higher frequency, and you will become amazed by the miracles that start showing up in your life.

# AUTHORS' PERSONAL EXPERIENCES

*Danielle*

I thought I understood the Law of Vibration when I was first introduced to it, but thinking you know something and truly believing it are two different things.

I made a common error, thinking positive thoughts without feeling them. When I was exposed to the concept, I wanted to attract the good that I desired into my life just by making my thoughts positive. I forgot that I should mix belief and action together in order to see my dream become a reality.

The result was that when my wishes—thoughts—didn't materialize, I became frustrated. This feeling of frustration was then compounded with anger, anxiety, and desperation. It seemed the more I tried, the worse things got.

It is undeniably true that positive thoughts alone won't manifest anything into your life.

Thinking positive is crucial, and it is the first step toward achieving what you want, yes, but positive thinking without the feeling of deep belief, without faith, has no power.

And of course, all this feeling needs to be accompanied by aligned action. You must not forget that energy is great, but tactical action steps are also required in order to move you toward the good that you want.

Only when this distinction became clear did I finally notice things begin to change. When I understood that my feelings control the vibration I am in, I made a point of becoming more consciously aware of my thoughts. And I started paying closer attention to what they led me to feel.

In summary, when you make the decision to try something new or move toward a goal not yet attained, you'll have certain thoughts of fear and doubt come up. But know that you have a choice as to whether you accept them or reject them. You can choose to feel that you are going to succeed or, you can choose to feel doubt and fear and perhaps the anxiety of impending failure. Make sure you are clear on your intention to succeed.

If, for example, you only tap into mediocre, listless energy phrases such as *I'll try,* you may start down the path of the new task or experience but without deep belief and faith, chances are you won't succeed. Replace *I'll try* with *I will.* It's not the absence of fear that will make you succeed, but the presence of faith. You may feel afraid when facing the unknown, and that's okay; it simply means you are moving yourself out from your comfort zone, and that is where growth happens. But, no faith? That will be sure to keep success at bay.

When my husband and I decided to move from Brazil to Portugal, there was only one thought in our minds: that of absolute success. Nothing anyone could tell us would have any negative effect on our belief that all the good we desired we would encounter by moving to Portugal. Nothing anyone could have said to us could have made us abandon the crazy idea of giving up everything we had to go on this adventure, to live into this dream.

We sold the few things we had. We quit our jobs. And we bought our airline tickets without even knowing if we would succeed in securing employment once we got there. We arrived in Portugal on a Sunday and were welcomed by some relatives and invited to stay with them. The very next day, my husband was hired to work on the construction site of a shopping center in town. Fifteen days later, we moved into our own place—a rental, yes—but ours nonetheless. Things from there on went well, and here we are today. Life is beautiful.

This is faith: to believe and act on something you cannot see, hear, smell, taste or touch, but to do so because you believe in its success.

And yes, at times we felt fear, but our faith in success was always stronger. And it is the strength of this faith that attracted to us all the good we were seeking. Why?

Because we became a vibrational match to the things we wanted. We were vibrating at the very same frequency of that which we desired.

So, you see, long before I had consciously been exposed to the Law of Vibration, I experienced it by allowing my desire to drive me into action. I attracted what I wanted to attract.

Now that I truly understand the Law of Vibration, miracles are constantly apparent in my life. All the people, resources, and circumstances I need to bring my dreams to fruition appear to me. I watch my conscious thoughts, I make gratitude lists, and I train myself to keep my frequency high. Feeling grateful has become a habit. The most important thing is that I feel good, and I am deeply grateful for feeling this way.

## Katerina

*The Law of Vibration? What you broadcast into the universe is what you get back? What kind of new age, hippy-spiritual mumbo jumbo is this?*

Those were my thoughts when I was originally introduced to the Law of Vibration. Okay, okay, yes—I had heard that Einstein and other Nobel award-winning scientists had proven that all matter is simply a form of energy, and that particles vibrate, but what the heck did that have to do with me?

If you're having a tough time with this concept, don't feel bad. Simply know that you're not alone. But, what we have described above as it relates to vibration and our ability as people to vibrate at different frequencies is absolutely law. And, as we indicated, the frequency you are vibrating at is what helps to determine your level of success in manifesting the life that you desire.

I had an interesting experience with the Law of Vibration a few years back. Having dreamt of being a television host since a child, when I made the decision to switch careers and move from the finance sector into media, I unknowingly shifted my vibration to a higher frequency state. Because of the joy felt in finally making the decision to honor my soul and pursue my childhood dream, my entire being was radiating. Unbeknownst to me, I was *vibrating high*.

At the time, I was living in Toronto, but I decided that Los Angeles, the mecca of media, was where I needed to be. On a random day in July, I was scheduled to take a flight from Toronto to Los Angeles. Although I typically flew business class, I wanted to be prudent with my money, so I had booked an economy class ticket. But before leaving the house for the airport, a thought crossed my mind: *I would really love to fly business class.*

When I got to the airport, I decided to see if a flight upgrade was available. I was told that yes, there were seats available, but that the cost to upgrade would be $1450. The flight itself cost me only $380 so I figured no, I didn't want to upgrade for over four times the cost. Economy class it was.

Although I was a little disappointed, I didn't allow myself to dwell on that disappointment. I instead proceeded to the gate, still quite content and excited about my flight to LA. I wasn't discouraged by the lack of ability to upgrade my ticket, I simply remained positively focused on the ensuing trip. I was vibrating high.

While sitting in the waiting area, I suddenly heard my name being called over the loud speaker, "Passenger Katerina Cozias, please come to the gate 12A ticket counter."

*Hmm,* I thought. *I wonder what this is all about?*

Upon walking up to the counter, the flight attendant looked at me and said, "Ms. Cozias, the flight is oversold."

*Oh no,* I thought.

And then she continued with, "We are going to have to upgrade you to business class."

You see, my desire to travel business class was fulfilled. Because that is how the universal Law of Vibration operates. Be clear on the *what* and let the universe figure out the *how*. Your job is simply to get yourself into a high vibration and stay there.

Call it *source energy*, call it *the universe*, call it *infinite intelligence*, call it *God*, call it whatever you will, but know that it has the power to respond to our desires. And when we are vibrating at a high frequency, the Law of Vibration invokes the Law of Attraction, and what we desire is simply attracted to us. Vibrate high and get ready to receive.

The universe rewarded me with exactly what I wished for, a business class flight. Because even upon feeling the disappointment of not having been able to book the upgrade myself, I chose not to sit in that disappointment but instead concentrated my attention on the positive feelings that the ensuing visit to Los Angeles was creating within me.

Do not be worried about the how: How will I get it? How will it come? How will I pay for it? Simply identify and be clear about the what: What do I want?

If you make a conscious effort to focus your thoughts and direct them toward seeing the positive instead of the negative, you will keep yourself in a higher vibrational frequency. In this state, be clear on what you want. Trust that the universe has your back, then just sit back and let the Law of Vibration and universal forces deliver on the how.

# CONCEPTS TO REMEMBER

*Use this space to highlight your favorite insights from this chapter*

- 

- 

- 

- 

- 

-

# 7

# Awareness

## WHAT DO YOU NOTICE AROUND YOU?

Our explanations are intended to increase your level of awareness and to help you connect with your inner self. The more self-connected you are, the more connected with the universe's infinite power you will be.

Everything you need, all the abundance you have ever asked for, all the good that you desire—all of it already exists. You live in an abundant world. All that is missing is to be aware of what state you are in and do what you need to shift to a place where more of what you want will naturally start to flow toward you.

The higher the degree of awareness you maintain, the more quickly you will tune in to your thoughts and feelings in a way that will allow you to shift to a higher frequency, thus accelerating your ability to manifest what you want.

By developing your sense of awareness, you will come to recognize that:

- We are all connected.
- The vibration you hold has the ability to affect other people's lives.

When people are aware of their oneness with Source, they feel connected to the universal force field, and they foster more confidence in the fact that the universe is supporting them. Awareness allows them to more easily identify opportunities, to more effectively magnetize people who can help them. They become more in tune with their own intuition, their internal guidance system. They know how to allow the universe to work for and through them. This is connection.

It is argued that human beings are the only species that can tune in to their internal selves; however, all animals are connected to Source. Animals survive largely on instinct. When threatened, they fight or flee. Most animals aren't equipped with higher faculties, such as reason, imagination, or any sense of aspiration. Animals survive because they simply react on instinct during times of peril.

Our ancestors had to trust those same fight or flight instincts to protect themselves from the dangers of their era, but as the human race evolved, human beings further developed their ability to think. They developed the ability to choose between *reacting* and *responding* to situations. People have the ability to consciously choose how to behave, but by default, many still react to situations rather than respond to them.

An example of people tending to react versus respond is when they find themselves stuck in traffic. Almost every driver has gotten into some sort of minor accident, at times because they chose to react versus respond.

When cut off by another driver, do you react or respond? Do you get angry, frustrated, or shout things at the other car? Do you lose control? Do you allow the circumstances to control you?

When you are operating at a low level of awareness, you allow circumstances to dictate your actions. You become the victim. When you respond instead of reacting, however, you are in control of yourself and of your circumstances. When you respond, you notice your reaction, or impending reaction, but you pause, take a breath, and consider the situation before acting. This puts you in control.

*When you react, you are giving away your power. When you respond,*
*you are staying in control of yourself.*

~ Bob Proctor

Awareness allows you to notice what you are noticing, and notice what you are not noticing. Ask yourself: *Where have I been directing my energy? What have I noticed, or failed to notice?*

Universal energy always flows toward whatever you give your attention to. For example, if you want more money but are constantly thinking of how deeply in debt you are, your energy is focused on the debt rather than on wealth creation. And so, you remain in debt.

If you want more money to flow into your experience, you must become aware of what thoughts you are thinking. In order to have money flow your direction, you must think abundant thoughts. Think wealth, riches, abundance, and prosperity. Literally envision your bank account accumulating cash. But most people who want or need money do just the opposite. They focus on the lack of cash in their bank accounts. And thus, lack of cash becomes their reality.

Are you failing to notice your own habitual thought patterns?

*The range of what we think and do is limited by what we fail to notice. And because we fail to notice, there is little we can do to change until we notice how failing to notice shapes our thoughts and deeds.*

~ R.D. Laing

Take a moment to become aware of your most common thoughts. Now, choose one behavioral pattern you would like to change. Perhaps you're the type of person who flips off the neighboring driver in traffic. Or maybe while scrolling through your social media feeds, you are the type of person who comments negatively on people's posts.

Commit now to stepping into awareness and notice the direction of your thoughts and your actions. This will allow you to more diligently mitigate your own negative and animalistic reactionary responses. Take back control of not only your circumstances but your life as well!

Commit to awareness. Commit to responding versus reacting. Commit to taking a breath and staying calm no matter what the situation. Use the power of thought to be aware of and control your own actions. Commit to remaining centered, calm, and serene. In time, and with practice, responding will become your default setting. By consciously choosing to respond versus react, you will systematically shed yourself of unnecessary hardship.

Your mind is like fertile soil, and fertile soil nourishes whatever is planted. If you plant toxic weeds, the soil will nourish them, and you will find yourself with a garden full of weeds. If you plant nutritious vegetables and healthy fruit trees, the soil will just as readily nourish that. You get to choose what you want to plant in the garden of your own mind. Our suggestion is that you choose wisely.

In summary, remember that anything you give your energy and attention to will grow. You get to choose whether you want to live in a world that reflects poverty or abundance. So, don't be shy. Nourish, really nourish, positive thoughts and become clear on what you want to see manifest in your life.

Listen to the inner voice that prompts you. It is prompting you in the direction of happiness and prosperity. That voice is your broader self, reminding you that you are an important part of creation and that you deserve all the goodness that exists for you. Become aware of your feelings as they pertain to your abundance—or lack thereof. Commit to directing good feelings and thoughts toward the things you desire. Become aware of your oneness with Source. Then, allow the universe to work for you.

# EXERCISE

Think back to a time that you were in a situation and didn't know how it would play out. You may have been anxious and stressed, but in the end, everything went well. Afterwards, you may have through to yourself: *If I had known that everything would turn out all right, I wouldn't have been so afraid.*

For example, students often become anxious before an exam. They spend sleepless nights worrying and at times even experience negative health issues, all caused by the fear of not knowing how things are going to play out. However, after they take the exam, if the test scores come back high, all the psychosomatic concerns disappear.

What things are you worrying about? How can an adjustment in your thought process and an awareness of your feelings lead to a more comfortable state in the moment?

*Calmness of mind is one of the beautiful jewels of wisdom. It is the result of a long and patient effort in self-control. Its presence is an indication of ripened experience and of a more than extraordinary knowledge of the laws and operations of thought.*
~ James Allen

1. Identify a time when you were hyper-anxious about an upcoming event, but in the end, all went well.

2. Identify the level of awareness you could have tapped into so you could better direct your energy toward the outcome you wanted.

3. Read the chapter on "Serenity" in James Allen's masterful book, *As a Man Thinketh*. Read this every day, twice a day, in the morning when you wake up and at night before you go to bed. These words of wisdom will soon shift the way you sustain your calmness of mind during tough times. In that serene state, you will become more aware and see more clearly how you have the power to shape your own life experience.

# AUTHORS' PERSONAL EXPERIENCES

*Danielle*

There was a time in my life when all I did was react: react to people, react to circumstances, react to God. In my mind, I thought that the difficulties I faced existed to make me feel like *life didn't like me at all*—I was really lost, and I did not know how to deal with all the negativity showing up in my life. At that point, I was subconsciously nourishing the negative. I couldn't see the good anywhere, in anyone, or in anything. At a certain point, I became really angry with life.

You see, although I hadn't realized it at the time, I was focusing my attention on the things I didn't want instead of on the things I did want. My thoughts were solely focused on the mean people and difficult situations I was experiencing. Because of this focus, those people and situations did not change. Although I wanted kind people in my world, I was directing my attention to just the opposite. Expecting things to go wrong or be difficult simply became my default state.

Whenever somebody tried to speak to me about the importance of correct thinking in pursuit of abundance I would listen quietly, respectfully, but in my mind, I used to think to myself: *I don't see abundance anywhere, for anybody—and even less so for myself.*

I was angry, and anger is what I planted in the fertile soil of my precious subconscious mind. As we mentioned above, it's important to remember that the subconscious mind treats all thoughts, good or bad, with the same care and nurturance. In my case, my poor life experience was simply a reflection of the fruit produced by my negative thinking.

Only after I made a conscious decision to become more aware of my thoughts and feelings did I notice that I was giving energy to the very things I didn't want. But because the energy was directed to them, it was those negatives that I was living: poor health, financial stress, angry people, lack of opportunity, and overall bad situations.

I proceeded like this until I simply couldn't continue any longer. It was time to make a change. Finally, when my awareness evolved, I began to see things differently. My perception changed, and I started to see things I hadn't seen before. Good things.

I chose to begin to respond instead of reacting. In time, consciously responding instead of subconsciously reacting became a habit. Now, when things happen, I can analyze the facts and make decisions more accurately than I used to because it's as if I've turned off the autopilot setting. I realized that I could be in control of my life and move toward what I wanted. And wow, was that liberating!

The quote above from James Allen's book, *As a Man Thinketh,* is from my favorite chapter in his book, "Serenity." It played a pivotal role for me during this transition from reacting to responding. Through the repetitive reading of these words of wisdom, little by little, things began to make sense. The more I put those words into practice, the more I became aware of the instances where I was responding versus reacting. And because of this, I started to notice real changes taking place with respect to my present circumstances and the mastery of my own thoughts.

I feel a sense of calm now knowing that it is simply up to me to hone my own awareness and willingness to respond instead of reacting. This is the direct correlation between cause and effect and how thoughts really do turn into things.

## Katerina

*Awareness,* just like many of the concepts in this book, may sound vague. In fact, it may even sound silly in its simplicity. *Of course, we are aware,* you might be thinking. We are aware we are on planet Earth. We are aware we are male or female. We are aware of what we ate for breakfast this morning. But the point here is, are you really *Aware?*

Aware with a capital A? Aware of how you are feeling, aware of the dominant pattern of your thoughts?

The importance of being aware of how you are feeling and in turn, directing your thoughts to match your desired state of emotion, plays a huge part in how your world unfolds around you.

I notice the truth of this when I take conscious steps to be aware of how I feel. On days where I jump out of bed with no time to collect my thoughts or set my intentions, I feel as if life is just throwing challenges in my direction. On most of those days, I react rather than respond. If the woman in the car in front of me on my drive to work is taking her time and misses a green light—which of course results in my missing the green light—I typically get angry and start honking the horn. I'm reacting.

But, on days when I take a few minutes to center myself in the morning before starting my day—fifteen minutes of meditation, writing ten things I am grateful for, and saying a little prayer for guidance and direction—I notice that my awareness of thought is more attuned. If I were to find myself in that same traffic jam, I would easily become aware and assess the situation instead of automatically falling into the act of reacting negatively and harshly.

Because I was consciously aware prior to responding, I might think a thought like: *Perhaps she was on the phone and got distracted, or perhaps she was early for her appointment and didn't feel the need to rush. Perhaps she had just last week gotten a speeding ticket and didn't want to chance that again.*

Instead of reacting, I would simply allow myself to step into a place of calm, becoming aware that there may be a multitude of reasons she missed the light. I would become aware of my reality, which was that I was now stuck at a red light and there was nothing that I could do about it. So, there are two choices: to become mad, angry, frustrated or to take a nice deep breath and scan the sides of the road for a beautiful tree or happy pedestrians.

When we tap into awareness, we are more likely to sense when anger or negativity is ready to overtake us. In that moment, we can choose to respond differently. We can choose to respond, not react. Awareness of your own personal emotions is key. Try to tune in to those on a daily basis and know that in time, this practice will help to build up your muscles of awareness and assist to create a more peaceful, serene, calm, and happy life experience.

# CONCEPTS TO REMEMBER

*Use this space to highlight your favorite insights from this chapter*

- 

- 

- 

- 

- 

-

# 8

# Your Infinite Source of Supply

**WHEN YOU DEAL WITH THE INFINITE, NEVER EXPECT TO GET LESS THAN WHAT YOU OFFER.**

People who have been raised with feelings of lack or limitation typically pass those same concepts on to the next generation. It's common to hear children asking their mother to buy a new toy and for the mother to respond with: *I can't afford it or I haven't got enough money.* It's common to hear someone say they want to buy a new house but they can't because they can't afford it. Or to hear children tell their friends that their parents told them not to share their lunch because there's not enough food at home.

You too may have been surrounded with messages of lack or scarcity when you were growing up. Perhaps you grew up in a household where scarcity statements were common:

- *We don't have enough money for that.*
- *There isn't enough for gifts.*
- *If you eat all the cookies in the jar, I won't buy any more.*
- *Don't use your colored pencils for fun—save them to do your homework because you might use them up.*

Those are the types of statements that build up a mental sense of limited supply. Those are the types of statements that tend to get passed on from generation to generation and can have a huge effect on how you show up in the world.

Childhood impressions of limitation—limited money, food, cookies, colored pencils—will grow in meaning and begin to expand into other areas of life as people age. Because these messages are ingrained so deeply into the subconscious, their limiting nature can and typically does affects a person's aspirations of being, doing, or having more: more money, more love, more life.

The universe itself is infinitely abundant, but ego often blinds humans to this fact. Because people feel fear and embody scarcity consciousness, they are often kept from recognizing another universal truth: the more you give, the more you receive.

*Amateurs compete; professionals create.*
~ Author unknown

The day human beings stop striving for individual gain is the day the world will change for the better. Everybody has the right to live in abundance because we are all abundant beings. In fact, we live in an abundant universe, one that is ready to provide us with anything we want. All we need to do is line up with the vibration of that which we want.

If you stop and pause for a moment, you'll realize that abundance is a universal default state. There are countless leaves on countless trees, infinite grains of sands strewn across beautiful beaches, and a myriad of birds flying across our vast skies. Abundance in ideas is perhaps the greatest example of all. For when you focus on finding solutions and creating opportunities, be assured that ideas will flow and you will be led to your ultimate solution.

It comes down, once again, to the importance of choosing your thoughts. It is your thoughts that influence your decisions and your actions—and thus, your results.

The truth is that the person who would like to buy a house but feels they don't have the money for it simply needs to remember that all that exists in the universe—from the most ethereal gas to the most apparently solid matter—is only energy. Money is simply energy. And it is all around. It is accessible even if it doesn't seem like it in the moment. The missing link therefore, is not the lack of cash; rather it is the lack of decision. You must first *decide* to purchase a house. For it is only once you decide, that opportunities will open up to point you in the direction of the resources required to make that purchase.

If you are being held back by the limiting belief of scarcity, know that once you make the decision to go after your desire, the resources you require will appear.

If you need money, be open to the many ways the money might show up. Release yourself from the anxiety of having to come up with it yourself and leave yourself open to the possibility of receiving it from other sources. The money you need might show in the form of a lucky lottery win. Perhaps a retired aunt might gift you with some money. But most likely, you may be introduced to someone who may offer you a new income generating opportunity.

By getting clear on what you want and then deciding with that clarity to move forward in that direction, you will receive the divine support you need. All the ideas, people, or opportunities required will appear to help you manifest that which you most truly desire, if you truly believe.

Don't be discouraged by the seeming lack of resources today. Trust that what you want is making its way to you, just as you are making your way to it. Of course, make sure to do what you can in tactical action to help bring the manifestation about. Find a real estate agent, spend an afternoon visiting an open house, flip through some home decor magazines. Allow yourself to become emotionally connected to the feeling of buying a new home, but also take the steps you need to make it happen.

> *Don't give me the facts, give me the truth. The facts are always changing.*
> ~ Patricia Shambrook

Now, we would like to invite you to dive deep into your own memories of past events. Let's see if we can help you to find evidence of something similar, of a time where things you thought were a lost cause or situations you assumed were doomed to fail turned out well at the eleventh hour.

We want you to look for evidence of times where things turned out well, even if at first you were concerned. For example:

- A solution to a problem you felt was unsolvable materialized out of the blue.

- The money you required to take that trip home shows up after you made the decision to visit your family.

- All the conditions required to buy that apartment of your dreams, the one you thought was out of your reach, suddenly lined up in a way that allowed you to get it.

> *Empty pockets never held anyone back.*
> *Only empty heads and empty hearts can do that.*
> ~ Norman Vincent Peale

Decision is crucial. It is what allows you to start to control your circumstances.

From the job you currently have to the amount of money in your bank account, everything is the result of past decisions you have made or haven't made. Remember, not making a decision is actually making a decision. It is the decision of inactivity.

> *Once you make a decision, the universe conspires to make it happen.*
> ~ Attributed to Ralph Waldo Emerson

There is a superior universal power that flows to you and through you. This power fuels the use of your higher mental faculties and allows you to tap into its inexhaustible energy and give form to the things you want. Each person is equipped with these higher faculties, which include will, reason, perception, imagination, intuition, and memory.

Ideas, inspirations, and innovative creation arise out of the molding of this energy, out of the molding of thought. The only thing that is required from you is that you pay attention to your thoughts. Be clear on what you want, and then listen for the ideas, listen for the inspiration.

To truly accelerate the manifestation process, however, you must pair commitment together with decisive action. One cannot succeed without the other. When you decide to do something, you must commit yourself to the idea.

People will often say *yes, I make decisions,* but when you look at their results, you don't see any evidence of real progress.

Saying that you decide to do something with your conscious mind is not the same as truly committing to your vision through the use of deep feeling and faith. Emotion is the language of the subconscious mind. And it is through the power of the subconscious mind that the magic happens.

Commitment takes decision making to a deeper level. Commitment is what enables you to become emotionally involved with an idea. It facilitates your ability to really *feel, at the deepest level of your being, as if what you want has already appeared.*

All day long you can tell yourself: *I've decided I want to produce and sell handcrafted objects because I love creating beautiful memorabilia,* but until you become truly committed to the idea, distractions abound. Only once you commit to your decision will you take steps to really see it come to fruition. The power of decision coupled with commitment will move you forward in the production of those handcrafted objects.

Decision plus commitment is the formula that motivates you to take action toward your goal. That is when results are created, irrespective of outside circumstances, such as the current economic conditions of the marketplace. When you are committed, current lack and limitation no longer stand as barriers.

Every one of us is a unique expression of this universal power. There is no beginning and no end to energy. You are part of the universe and the universe is part of you. Everything you need is already within you—the infinite source of supply is in your own mind. And it can be harnessed through your ability to think the way you want to think.

> *My mind is a center of Divine operation. The Divine operation is always for expansion and fuller expression and this means the production of something beyond what has gone before, something entirely new, not included in past experience, though proceeding out of it by an orderly sequence of growth. Therefore, since the Divine cannot change its inherent nature, it must operate in the same manner in me; consequently, in my special world, of which I am the center, it will move forward to produce new conditions, always in advance of any that have gone before.*
>
> ~ Thomas Troward

In order to create what you want to create, begin with a definite goal in mind. Working toward a clearly defined goal keeps you motivated, stretches your capabilities, and expands your consciousness. Goal setting is imperative because it helps identify what you need to accomplish in order to pursue a definite course of action. Goals provide clarity on how to achieve the things you want to do and have.

Let's look at how goals integrate into the grand picture of life:

- Your Purpose: Defines *why* you are here. It is your mission. Purpose is what drives you to fulfill your truest objective.

- Your Vision: Keeps you on track in the pursuit of all that you came here to pursue. It is the act or power of imaginatively creating and eagerly anticipating that which is to come.

- Your Goals: Are the constant tactical activity that keep you moving forward, from one point to another as you move along your intended path.

We can liken *purpose* to a GPS system: it keeps you on track and gives your life direction. Your vision drives your journey. It includes creating a framework for the experiences you wish to have. Your goals are what keep you moving. Your goals ensure you are always expanding, moving from point A to point B, always in the direction of your vision and purpose.

You might know what your purpose is. You may be clear on your vision. But unless you have solid plans to execute, by way of defined goals, you will find yourself stuck.

Therefore, you must first decide what it is that you want to accomplish and then commit to getting there. This is why goal setting is so important. Without goals, change simply does not happen. This is why the majority of people seem to live a life that can be likened to a cork bobbing in the ocean. Because they neglect to aim for anything definite, they simply remain stuck in their present circumstance.

If you are not used to setting goals, don't fear, start small. Begin to set small, easily achievable goals. Hitting a goal and completing the task will create forward momentum and soon you will be able to set bigger and bigger goals. The more goals you successfully hit, the more positive transformational change you can expect to experience in your life. Know also that the bigger you set your goal, the greater the opportunity for self-growth and for a richer, more complete life experience.

Everything you need is already within you. You have the power to think, and thought is the most potent force on earth. Thought is a powerful tool, equally available to everyone. Thus, through the power of thought, you have everything you need to truly achieve what you want.

Thought allows you to tap into the unlimited supply of the subconscious mind. All you need to do is become clear on what it is that you want to have.

You now know that your mental programming either supports you in growth or it leads you to atrophy. You now know that you have the power to become aware of your own thoughts and to replace negative ones with positive ones. You now know that you create your own reality based on your energetic frequency and the congruency of vibrational alignment between yourself and the things you want. And you now know that there is access to an infinite source of supply within you.

If you are not living the life you know you really want to live, ask yourself: *Why not?* Do you want a better job? Then start looking for one. Set a goal to look for ten new employment opportunities a week and stick to that, week after week, until you find one that better suits your needs. Be clear on the type of job you want and the style of work environment you want to spend your day in. Be clear on all the details, and then begin to become emotionally involved with that idea.

Focus your thoughts and attention on that vision, using your imagination to create it first in your mind. Then, using your feelings and emotions, really step into the preverbal essence of what it would be like to live that perfect day.

Your subconscious mind will take the order that is churning in your conscious mind and start to magnetize the right opportunity to you, and you to it. Be clear on what you want, and then take actionable steps that will help you to get there. But remember, although yes, action is important, the expectation of achieving the desired outcome is equally important. This is where most people fail. They focus solely on action to the exclusion of true belief.

Be cautious, because even when forward movement is imminent, negative mental conditioning will try to pull you back. Through conscious awareness of your thoughts and feelings, you can mitigate this and choose to replace negative thoughts with more positive ones. Over time the more positive, constructive thinking will become your default state.

So, don't be shy, give yourself mental permission to dream. Live the life you really want to live. Because remember, there is indeed an infinite source of supply. All you need to do is use the power of thought to tap into it.

*When riches begin to come, they come so quickly, in such great abundance, that one wonders where they have been hiding during all those lean years.*

~ Napoleon Hill

# EXERCISE

1. Make a list of ten things you want to do or accomplish and commit now to making them a reality.

2. For each item, identify what actions steps you need to take in order to achieve it.

3. For each item, set a clearly defined time frame for its execution and completion.

4. Answer this question: *What do I really want?* Are the ten things you listed above in alignment with these wants?

# AUTHORS' PERSONAL EXPERIENCES

*Danielle*

It became crystal clear to me that all the resources I need are already inside of me. This is because I came to recognize the truth about how our thoughts mold our reality, how the universe operates, and about our role as co-creators in our own life experience.

When you understand this, all doubts and fears disappear, and life begins to unfold much more smoothly than before. Instead of allowing myself to be controlled by circumstances, I now create my own. I know now that my role in the universe is to do what I've got to do, and I let the universe provide me with all the resources I need.

*Katerina*

In this chapter, we're talking about an infinite source of supply. If you are anything like I used to be, you might be thinking: *Okay, if there is an infinite source of supply, then why isn't it infinitely sourcing me with all the goodness I want in my life?*

This was my thinking before I truly became acquainted with this material. It wasn't until I became aware of my own thoughts and perceptions that I realized I was tuning to lack because I was choosing not to notice abundance. When I started focusing on the good in my life—my healthy body, my loving family, my many opportunities—I started to immediately experience better results in my life. Thoughts build thought momentum. Positive ones invite more positive ones and negative ones invite more negative ones.

The reason we say *there is infinite supply* is because energy is infinite. It simply exists. It is all around us, and when we take our thoughts, focus on an outcome, expect and believe that that outcome will come to pass, there is no alternative but for that outcome to materialize in physical form. So, if it is money you want, simply start noticing the abundance that is prevalent in your life rather than your lack of physical dollars in your wallet.

Shifting from scarcity-based consciousness to abundance-based consciousness will cause you to vibrate at and emit a higher frequency. By shifting to a higher vibrational frequency, you become a magnet for more good to flow into your experience.

Don't be frustrated with your current living conditions or financial situation. Start instead to shift to a feeling of gratitude for all that you do have. Recognize the benefit of having a roof over your head and a bed to lay your head down on. Train your mind to appreciate what you *do* have. Once you make the mental shift from lack to abundance, your frequency will raise and more and more abundance will start to flow into your life experience. Supply is infinite. Use the power of your mind to allow unlimited supply to flow to you.

# CONCEPTS TO REMEMBER

*Use this space to highlight your favorite insights from this chapter*

- 
- 
- 
- 
- 
-

# 9

# Attitude—The Magic Word

**ONE OF THE GREATEST DISCOVERIES OF HUMAN BEHAVIOR IS YOUR ABILITY TO DETERMINE YOUR OWN ATTITUDE.**

What you broadcast to the universe is what you get back. Broadcast positivity and you will experience positivity. Broadcast negativity and you will experience negativity.

How much of a role does your own attitude play in all this? It plays a huge role! For it is your attitude that determines the intensity of the energy you bring to any task or project. Attitude is a settled way of thinking or feeling that is reflected in your behavior.

Notice the many ways human beings relate to each other. Body language, based on your attitude, speaks volumes. What does your body posture communicate? Does it reflect proactivity, self-confidence, and strong energy? Or, are you coming across as tired, unmotivated, and someone with low self-esteem? Your attitude plays a huge role in the frequency you hold and the vibration you project.

How do you verbally interact with people? Do you compliment someone whom you've just met or are you more reserved with your words? How do you shake their hand? Is your handshake strong, warm, and inviting, or is it loose and cold?

What about the tone of your voice? Is it pleasing, clear, enthusiastic? Or, is it harsh and abrasive?

When was the last time you paid attention to your facial expressions? What do the various looks on your face convey to other people? Eye contact has more power than you think. Have you ever noticed that when you smile without the feeling of happiness, your eyes don't reflect the upturn of your mouth? When you are truly happy, however, one of the first parts of your face to show your real smile is your eyes. Your attitude is projected through your physicality, all day, every day.

Attitude is incredibly important. The attitude you project affects the state that you are in, and it is this state that then affects the type of interaction you have with others. Remember, in order to achieve what you want, you need to embody the feeling of having already achieved it. Your attitude plays a big role in helping you do this.

If you are a student and you want better results at school, consider what attitude you bring to school with you every day. What thinking does your behavior reflect? Do you believe you can do well in a given subject? Remember, in order to achieve the result you want to achieve, you need to see yourself already in possession of the good that you desire.

Want to accelerate your results at school? Study hard yes, because right action is certainly important, but don't forget to adjust your thoughts and attitude in order to tune in to the frequency of *good grades.*

If you are a student and you would like to do better in school, we recommend following a procedure similar to the one outlined here:

- Find a comfortable chair to sit in and relax your body.

- Hold the image of what you want in your mind. See yourself taking a test or completing an assignment and envision the best result possible.

- Hold that vision in your mind daily and go about your day embodying the feeling and the excitement of receiving the result you want.

- Take aligned action. Tactical action is a must, so in addition to holding the vision and the feeling of the *win,* make sure to do your best to prepare.

Adjust your attitude to do whatever it takes to move you toward that end goal—for example, double your study time, join a group study session, or book an extra tutorial.

Be clear on the outcome you want, adjust your attitude to one of excitement for the task at hand, and really see, feel, and embody the emotions of having already received the result you want.

Suppose you are in sales or are the owner of your own business. Do you want to be regarded as the industry expert in your field? Do you want to actually achieve results that would make that indisputable? It's natural to want to win at life. Achieving career success in a way that aligns with personal fulfillment is a great way of augmenting your life's experience.

To help accelerate your results, start to mentally live into the vision of the person you want to become. Once you have a clear image of yourself as the undisputed industry expert in your field, bring those traits into your current now:

- Start to dress the way a successful entrepreneur dresses.
- Frequent the venues successful entrepreneurs frequent.
- Project confidence when you walk.

- Provide the best service you can render to your clients.
- Take steps to acquire any additional training or skills you might need in order to accelerate your results.

With the right attitude, you can achieve anything you want. Because remember, your attitude toward others and life will determine others' and life's attitude toward you.

That is why the father of the modern self-development movement, Earl Nightingale referred to attitude as *the magic word*. Cultivate a good attitude and trust that in time, the world will bend to deliver whatever it is you desire.

> *Attitude is the composite of your thoughts, feelings, and actions.*
> *Your attitude produces your results.*
> ~ Bob Proctor

Take a moment now to become aware of your current attitude toward life. Is it the attitude you want to have? Know that attitude can be voluntarily changed. You have the power to choose your own attitude. How fantastic!

Want to increase your chances of leveraging attitude in order to fuel forward momentum? The first step is to gain clarity on what areas of your life you wish to accelerate. Make a list of every aspect you want to improve.

If you don't know exactly how to get started, our suggestion is to make a list of successful people in each of the respective areas and identify what it is about their personalities that you resonate with.

Second, list all the aspects of your current personality and attitude that you wish to change in order to better align your mind and body with the achievement of each previously identified desire.

And finally, be specific in pinpointing what those aims are. For instance, do you desire more free time? Okay, but what does that look like? Be specific in what you would do with more free time. Would you spend more time with your family? Would you read more books on ways to improve your skill set or industry knowledge? Would you meet up with more people who have a proven level of success in your line of work? The universe responds to your every wish and desire, but only if you are very clear on the details.

Regardless of the goal, cultivating a positive attitude, one of excitement and expectancy, will make all the difference. Make a point of projecting a good attitude and experience for yourself how magical this word truly becomes.

# AUTHORS' PERSONAL EXPERIENCES

## *Danielle*

As was described in the chapter "Dispelling Limiting Beliefs," I had to replace my negative self-talk with positive self-talk. I had reached a point of frustration and severe anger, so I made a commitment to really embody new positive thoughts in order to change my subconscious self-image.

A good attitude coupled with action creates results. This is important to note. For even with a good attitude, you won't be able to experience change if you do not act to initiate it. By consciously choosing to change my attitude on a cellular level, I inadvertently adjusted my physical state while replacing my previously negative self-talk with more positive internal dialogue.

Under the old attitude paradigm, when I used to believe I lacked courage, my posture and body language reflected that belief. I was shy, I made no eye contact, my body was hunched over and seemingly closed off, and I moved clumsily instead of gracefully.

I was frustrated with my lack of success. So frustrated in fact, that one day I decided something drastically needed to change. I chose to test for myself how a shift in attitude might impact my life.

I started by replacing the negative thoughts with positive ones. I repeatedly told myself I was courageous and consciously adjusted my posture, my walk, and my stance to one that reflected more confidence. I took the initiative to compliment people instead of waiting for them to compliment me. I started making a point of establishing eye contact. I began sharing my ideas, even though at first this really didn't feel comfortable. But that's the idea. There's no growth in the comfort zone.

I was uncomfortable when I first started to do things differently until the point came when things started to shift in my favor because of this adjusted attitude and behavior. After some time, people's attitudes toward me started to change. I began to feel respected and even admired. For the first time in my life, I felt that others valued my opinion and that my presence was not only welcomed but requested. The magic lay in my attitude. At first, I pretended to be a confident person. Then, I simply was one.

The transition from *pretending* to *being* took place so smoothly and so unexpectedly that I can't even pinpoint the exact moment that I truly stepped into my most confident self. It simply happened. I didn't need to pretend anymore, to keep my thoughts in check, or make sure that my affirmations remained positive. I didn't need to pay attention to my body posture; it was already expressing confidence. When I needed to act the part, I didn't need to act anymore because I *was* the part. Maintaining a positive attitude had simply become a habit. Once I changed my attitude for the better, my results changed for the better.

## Katerina

I used to be a *glass half-empty* kind of person. I used to be the *yes, but* person, and the *but* was almost always followed by a negative statement, comment, concern, or fear. My life reflected this poor attitude. My life was half empty.

When I became acquainted with many of the concepts we explore in this book, my level of awareness raised. I realized that I had the power to choose not only my thoughts but to choose the direction in which I wanted my life to go. I had a choice: to continue living as a responder to outside conditions or to begin to live my life on purpose. I came to realize that I could create the desired emotions and feelings on the inside, which would fuel more positive thinking and, in turn, reflect a better life experience.

*Attitude of mind*: it is one of the greatest secrets of all. Think about it: a person with a good attitude is always welcome. I decided to shift my attitude from one of fear and lack-based thinking to one of anticipation, excitement, and belief-based thinking. And that has made all the difference.

Now, when faced with a challenge, instead of thinking: *Great, just my luck*, I think: *okay, interesting, I wonder what this problem has to teach me? Get ready to grow Katerina, get ready to grow!* I take on that challenge with a game-like sense of interest and excitement. And you know what? Because of my shift in attitude, the problem gets mentally reframed as a fun puzzle to solve, rather than an overwhelming challenge to overcome.

Your attitude—the manner in which you choose to deal with things—is incredibly important. Remember, nothing is good or bad, or right or wrong, or left or right. It just is. The way you experience life simply depends on your perception of it. If you perceive something as being good, it will be good. If you perceive it as being bad, it will be bad. You have the ability to choose how you view life. Shift your attitude and notice the way life shifts for you.

# CONCEPTS TO REMEMBER

*Use this space to highlight your favorite insights from this chapter:*

- 

- 

- 

- 

- 

-

# 10

# The Influence of Mentors

**A MENTOR IS SOMEONE WHO SEES IN YOU SOMETHING YOU CANNOT SEE IN YOURSELF.**

Some of the greatest achievers throughout history had people of influence in their lives whose characters and personalities they emulated in the development of their own.

A mentor is an experienced or trusted advisor. A mentor can help provide information and knowledge, most importantly as it pertains to your own self-growth and expansion. Identify the people you admire and seek to spend time with them. When looking for a mentor, choose someone who inspires you, someone who will help to empower you to act on your ideas.

A wise mentor can play a pivotal role in your life. Typically, a mentor is someone who has lived through an experience you wish to live through or has hit a career milestone that you also wish to hit. Mentors share thoughts, ideas, and accumulated knowledge in a way that can help to more easily and fluidly reach your intended goal.

In many cases, a mentor can help to guide you beyond your perceived limitations, helping to heighten your curiosity and expand your thinking.

> *The delicate balance in mentoring someone is not creating them in your own image but giving them the opportunity to create themselves.*
> ~ Steven Spielberg

Clear thinking is king. And yet, most of society sorely misses the mark when it comes to the importance of thought and the thinking process.

Children are naturally creative, curious, imaginative, and inquisitive. As they grow into adults, they lose their connection to many of those qualities. Unfortunately for children, many parents, teachers, and other adults of influence lack patience. When a child asks a question, it is often met with impatience and perhaps some inadvertent judgment.

Without meaning to, many parents squelch the child's sense of wonder, or even worse, respond with an implication that denotes the child is silly for asking the question in the first place. When this happens, the child starts to lose their sense of wonder and begins to limit their own ability to think and question. As children age, they tend to think less and less for themselves and willingly lose their unique sense of self in order to fit in with others. Because of this, by adulthood, most people simply default to *a follow the crowd* mentality.

Let's ask ourselves, why is less than 10 percent of the global population experiencing wealth and abundance? Could it be because those who achieve big things had the courage to step away from the herd mentality and think for themselves?

*Thinking* is the master key to achieving what you want. And often, it's those people who have already achieved what you want to achieve that can help you get on the correct path. Success often hinges on getting the right advice or support from the right people.

When you work with a mentor, you benefit from learning from someone who has already reached the point you are trying to reach. They have already made the mistakes, learned the lessons, discovered what works and what doesn't. A mentor is someone who will be able to show you things that you might not have been able to see for yourself, someone who can provide a road map where perhaps there wasn't one before.

You must learn to assess situations from different perspectives. You must learn to explore every alternative in order to work from a place of possibility. A mentor can help you do this. Working with a mentor can help introduce you to a side of yourself you may not have met before. A mentor can help to bring to the surface the most creative, powerful, and unique parts of your personality.

*Know thyself.*
~ Socrates

Now, you may be wondering: *How does one go about finding a mentor?*

Find someone you want to be like, study that person, and then reach out to them to ask if they would be willing to mentor you. Our advice, however, is not to ask that person to be your mentor right off the bat, especially if the person is unknown to you. Rather, ask for an initial meeting, something informal, and come to the meeting from a place of service. What can you offer the prospective mentor so that the situation doesn't become *all about you?*

Once the meeting is over, evaluate how you feel. Do you want to spend more time with this person? Do you feel they'll be an asset to you? If so, reach out to them with the ask, and then let the relationship develop organically.

So, go ahead, find your mentor. Ask questions. Learn all you can learn. Align with people who will support you throughout your development, both personally and professionally. And watch the good it can bring.

# AUTHORS' PERSONAL EXPERIENCES

*Danielle*

As I described in my opening notes of dedication, I consider Américo Vieira my first mentor—and he still is—because he invited me to view life in a way that I had never experienced before. Through the many in-depth conversations he and I have had, he's taught me valuable lessons and shared wonderful and wise insights, approaches, and perspectives. He really knows how to offer food for thought.

At the beginning, it took some time for me to absorb what he was trying to share with me, but like a seed that takes its time to sprout, all his words of wisdom simply needed their space to gain meaning in my mind.

I am so grateful that the universe put us on the same path. He not only saw potential in me, he taught me to appreciate things in myself that I had never appreciated in the past. Because of the whole new world he introduced me to, I was open to seeking even more mentors. I found another great human being, who, through his generosity in sharing all his knowledge and wisdom, helped me to unleash my infinite potential: thought leader and transformational life coach, Bob Proctor.

Through his vast experience in the world of personal development and his more than fifty-five years of study of the human mind and behavior, Bob's teachings helped me to better understand the metamorphosis that was taking place within myself.

Words cannot express the joy that I feel for now being aware of, and present to, my own essence and true self. Mentors, therefore, have played a huge part in my personal self-development and transformational growth.

As children, we are taught so many facts and figures, but rarely are we ever exposed to how to get in touch with ourselves. And yet, honing this very ability is crucial for us to relate to the outside world in a way that will be of benefit to all. The better you know yourself, the better you know and can relate to others.

## *Katerina*

Finding a mentor is incredibly important. However, securing one is not always that easy. In many cases, although you need that person in your life, they do not need you in theirs.

So, how do you go about finding a mentor? In addition to the steps outlined above, here are a few more pointers for you.

Start by identifying the people in your chosen field of endeavor and make a list. List as many of the top achievers as you can. Then, narrow that list by singling out the ones whose work you truly admire—whose work ethic you most resonate with. With whom might you be most interested in spending time? Next, just jump in and approach them. Send them an email if you have their email address. Or, reach out to them on social media platforms as best you can.

A mentor can also be someone who you already know. If this is the case, terrific. But if the mentor you really desire is someone you feel may be out of your reach, don't despair. My advice is to seek ways to contact them anyway. Sure, they don't know you—yet. Perhaps they say yes. Perhaps they say no. Since the worst they can say is no, you have nothing to lose by trying.

My experience with most people is that they are typically flattered when approached. If they are not willing to fully take on the role of mentor, most of the time, they are at least willing to share some ideas or offer some advice that will get you pointed in the right direction.

Relationships are a two-way street. In order to receive, you must first give. When approaching a prospective mentor, offer something of value to them first, be it your time in assisting them or your thoughts on providing an alternative perspective for a project that they might be working on. You never know when your unique perspective might be just the alternate perspective they have been looking for.

Remember, life is a journey, one that is always more fun when filled with friends and mentors who are willing to come along for the ride.

# CONCEPTS TO REMEMBER

*Use this space to highlight your favorite insights from this chapter:*

- 

- 

- 

- 

- 

-

# 11

# The Power of Mastermind Groups

**LEVERAGE THE MIND POWER OF A TEAM TO HELP YOU GO FURTHER.**

Throughout this book, we have shared techniques, teachings, and ideas aimed at helping you unleash your infinite potential. We have asked you to:

- Get clear on your passion or purpose.
- Set a dream or big picture vision for your life.
- Cultivate awareness of your thoughts.
- Recognize that you have the power to shift your vibration.
- Decide and commit to your personal growth and expansion.

- Seek those who can help guide you along your journey.

This may sound overwhelming, but the good news is that you don't have to walk alone.

As a compliment to the internal work you will do on and for yourself, we recommend leveraging the power of a collective mind and teaming up with a group of individuals who are also dreaming big. We recommend joining or starting a mastermind group. Mastermind groups offer a combination of peer brainstorming, accountability, and support in a team setting to help you create the success you want.

Together, in the spirit of harmony, cooperation, and support you can be there for each other as you grow.

A common mistake that poor achievers make is to believe that they already know everything there is to know, that there's nothing to learn from others. Poor achievers have ideas but they typically fail to expand on those ideas. So, those ideas never come to fruition.

Say, for example, someone has an idea for an invention that can change thousands of lives for the better, but, they don't know how to execute the logistics of developing it, so they don't. Feeling the pressure, fear, and anxiety of going at it alone, they decide instead to shelf the idea and simply stop all creative thought. Because they stop here, the idea is forever lost, and the world is denied the creation of a product that could have been of benefit to many.

We want you to realize that you don't need to go at life alone. And you certainly don't need to know how to execute every detail of every piece of the development process. There are others who may have the knowledge you need. All you need to do is find them. Remember, you are not an island.

This is where a mastermind group becomes invaluable. Many of history's greatest achievers garnered success due to their participation in a mastermind group and their cooperation with other minds.

An example of someone who leveraged the power of an organized mastermind group in order to achieve incredible amounts of success was Henry Ford. From humble beginnings with no formal education, the odds of Henry Ford succeeding in life were slim. And yet, he was determined to make it, determined to see his idea of a horseless carriage come to pass.

Henry Ford recognized his limitations so he sought to befriend, and then collaborate with, minds greater than his own. He befriended the great Thomas A. Edison. He then went on to cultivate relationships with Harvey Firestone, John Burroughs, and Luther Burbank. Yes, Henry's achievements in life were a combination of his drive, dedication, and perseverance, but they were also due in large part to his strong association and interaction with the great and talented minds of the day.

In order to form your own strong mastermind group, all participants must commit to bringing to the group the best version of themselves. Participants must also understand that they are there to both give and receive. The Law of Giving and Receiving is a major staple of any mastermind group.

Imagine how you'd feel if you were invited to a dinner party where each person was instructed to bring a main dish, and you arrived empty handed. Would you feel comfortable tasting the others' dishes knowing you didn't bring anything? Probably not. But if you had come to the party with your own tasty dish, your appetite and willingness to share in the delights of all dishes would increase. It is the same thing with a mastermind group. If you share valuable insights and ideas, you will be more likely and willing to receive them from others.

Why is the mastermind group a master key for success? The key lies in the underlying principle of the compounding power of multiple minds. When two or more minds are brainstorming in a spirit of cooperation, they enter into a state known as *synergy*. Synergy takes place when two minds, working in perfect harmony and cooperation with each other, produce a superior thinking force, as if a third mind were cooperating with them. Simply said, think of it as 1 + 1 = 3.

By brainstorming, new ideas will seem to form from thin air as the combination of your respective ideas create completely new ones. This is one of the magnificent benefits of joining a mastermind group.

To create your own mastermind group, seek people with whom you would like to exchange ideas and discussion, and then allocate a certain time on a certain day, weekly or monthly, to meet and review each other's projects.

When looking for individuals to help make up the group, seek people you feel will have things of value to contribute. Positive attitudes are also recommended.

Another benefit of a mastermind group is that its team members can help to hold each other accountable, which ensures people stay on track with tasks they have committed to. If you form a mastermind group and leverage the respective skill sets of its members, don't be surprised to see yourself achieving results you had never expected to achieve.

Why go at life alone when you can do it with the support and structure of a team? When you have people supporting you and your dream, consistently encouraging you to keep striving forward, magical things start to happen. And so, go ahead, contact some people you feel you would like to learn from, share, and grow with, and watch the collective spirit of your mastermind group move you ever forward toward your dream.

# AUTHORS' PERSONAL EXPERIENCES

## *Danielle*

This very book is a result of a mastermind group—one that I am still a part of today.

Joining this group was one of the best decisions I have ever made. Due to the support and encouragement I received, I have grown so much as a person. Becoming a member of the group put me in contact with incredible, like-minded people who shared my drive and altruistic qualities.

Our meetings are very productive. We support each other, we offer constructive criticism, and we celebrate each other's wins. We work together to find ways to help each of us achieve our respective goals, always in cooperation and mutual appreciation of our like-minded drive. I feel energized every time we meet. Because of the mutual intent to show up as the best version of ourselves, the vibration generated becomes electric. I feel recharged, renewed, and like I've inhaled a powerful breath of fresh air after every meeting. Because of this high frequency, energy and ideas flow with ease and grace.

If you are not yet part of a mastermind group, I highly encourage you look for one to join, or better yet, start your own. Team up with like-minded high achievers and watch magnificent results start to flood your world.

## Katerina

As Danielle mentioned, this book is a result of conversations that took place during a mastermind meeting of a group that she and I are both part of.

At first, I was a little reluctant to join the group, since some of its members were not local, which meant we would have to hold our meetings online. Always a fan of in-person connections, the thought of online meetings seemed weird to me at first, but with the wonderful advancements in technology, our meetings came together seamlessly. The lack of physical proximity to one another turned out not to be an issue.

Although being able to physically be in a room together does have its benefits, don't feel restrained when starting your own mastermind group. If the people you would like to invite happen to live in different cities, or even different countries, do not let this be a barrier to starting it.

Napoleon Hill, in his classic book, *Think and Grow Rich*, touts the benefits and importance of the mastermind principle. So do Danielle and I, for we have experienced its benefits firsthand. And we would love for you to as well.

More minds are always better than one, and if those minds are aligned in common expectation for success, achievement, and prosperity for all, trust me when I say the sky is the limit.

# CONCEPTS TO REMEMBER

*Use this space to highlight your favorite insights from this chapter:*

- 

- 

- 

- 

- 

-

# Conclusion

*Rising Up From Mental Slavery: How to Unleash Your Infinite Potential* is intended to offer precise and powerful tools for those seeking to change their lives for the better.

In Chapter One, we invited you to ask yourself: *What's holding you back?* Irrespective of circumstance, financial conditions, or seemingly negative employment situations, you have access to the infinite potential that lies within you through the power of thought. The key is to garner awareness of these thoughts and to use them to identify the limiting beliefs that are currently holding you back.

Now is the time to take 100 percent responsibility for your life and your actions, for when you do, things will begin to change. Allow yourself to dream again, to dream with the limitlessness of a child. Seek to step into your purpose, and then build a vision around what the life of your dreams looks like. Know that you have the power to see it become a reality.

The desire for change, in any aspect of your life, stems from the calling of your own internal spirit. Spirit is always seeking expansion and fuller expression. The desire to express your true self, your true wants and needs, will always be present. To live a life of ease, grace, and flow, you must have the courage to honor that calling by following the truth of your heart. Listen to its whispers, listen to its leanings, listen to your intuition, for it is all there to guide you toward your highest good.

We have attempted to share the impactful messages in this book in ways that are simple to read and easy to understand. In addition to the information provided, one of the reasons we wanted to share our personal experiences was to help you to recognize that you are not alone in your quest for a more fulfilled and passionate life. We, as the authors, are no different from you. We have our struggles as well as our moments of glory.

By using the tools outlined in this book, we have experienced shifts in the way we see ourselves and thus, in the world that surrounds us. Had we not been exposed to all the principles in this book, we would never have achieved *our* dreams. But we have. And we continue to, knowing that the power lies within. And that, Dear Reader, is a most comforting thought.

We want you to know that the universe works in the most precise way. Everything you are experiencing is intended to point you towards growth. But it is up to you to recognize that it is your personal beliefs, thought patterns, and, yes, attitude, that create the momentum that will see you either rise in glory or continue to struggle in pain. You have the power to design the life that you want, and by doing so in the manner that is most aligned to your personal truth, you will not only benefit yourself but you will benefit those around you.

Time is our most precious commodity. And so, now is the time to get started. Don't wait any longer to step into all the abundance that is waiting for you. When you align yourself with the calling of your heart and your soul, magic truly abounds. Everything begins inside of you, and only you have the power to make it happen. Rise up now from mental slavery and unleash your infinite potential!

**To learn more about working with Katerina Cozias, to access her online programs, or to book Katerina to speak at your next event, please visit**

**KaterinaCozias.com**

**To learn more about working with Danielle Martins, to enlist her as your coach, or to book Danielle to speak at your next event, please visit**

**DanielleMartins.com**

# About the Authors

*Danielle Martins*

Danielle Martins is a Personal Branding Strategist, and Marketing Specialist with 26 years of experience (2024), consultant, mentor, workshop facilitator, entrepreneur, best-selling author, and international speaker.

Her specialty is helping entrepreneurs and book authors become industry leaders by strategically managing their Personal Brands so they can experience sustainable success.

Danielle's childhood and teenage years were not easy ones however, and by the time she reached adulthood, she felt that she had lost a part of herself. After some life-altering changes, she started to seek more deeply the true meaning of our existence. She sought to find out if emotional fulfillment was something available to her.

Absorbing as much knowledge as she could in the world of personal development and self-transformation, her big leap happened when she came across the work of the world-renowned philosopher, coach, and personal growth mentor, Bob Proctor.

As she applied his teachings, she witnessed firsthand the improvement of her results. Her goals became clearer, her focus narrowed, and little by little, her circumstances started to change for the better.

Danielle's unwavering dedication to personal growth and expansion has led her to a profound understanding of herself and her purpose. Now, leveraging this insight, she assists others in realizing their own aspirations. Spanning 27 countries, Danielle empowers professionals worldwide to become industry leaders, guiding them to uncover their authentic selves and harness their unique strengths to achieve their dreams.

For more about Danielle, please visit: DanielleMartins.com

## *Katerina Cozias*

Katerina is an international media expert, on-camera TV host, and professional speaker.

Born in Canada and currently residing in Los Angeles, as a professional on-camera personality, Katerina has participated in award show commentary and covered red carpet premieres for some of Hollywood's most prestigious events. As compliments to her strong skills as a producer and host, she has overseen the communications, media, and pitch strategies for several international brands across broadcast, print, digital, and social media platforms. As a speaker, she has presented in many of the world's most exciting cities, including, but not limited to: New York, Hong Kong, Moscow, Athens, Dubai, Cannes, Montreal, Monte Carlo, and Miami.

It was during her time in the air that she became acquainted with the world of personal development. Fascinated, Katerina started seeking content, listening to audio books, and reading material written by the many of the field's greats, including Napoleon Hill, Earl Nightingale, Thomas Troward, Tony Robbins, Jack Canfield, Marianne Williamson, and Les Brown. As her awareness of the incredible and highly underutilized potential and power of the human mind grew, the importance of better understanding concepts, such as *positive mental attitude, belief in self,* and the *power of thought* became personal passions.

Through the strategic cultivation of her own positive vibration and high frequency, she began attracting the people and circumstances necessary to achieve her goals. And achieve her goals she did. During her personal growth journey, one of the people who came into her life was Danielle Martins. At the time, Danielle was living halfway around the world, but an introduction via a mastermind group brought them together. They instantly connected and in time decided to collaborate on this book. That, Dear Reader, is exactly how the Law of Attraction and the Law of Vibration work.

And so, if you know you are meant to be living a more fulfilling life, have faith in yourself, believe in your vision, stay true to your goals, maintain the correct mental attitude, and trust that the right people will show up for you at just the right time.

Life is intended to be an excellent adventure. Get excited, for there are so many wonderful experiences ahead. The time is now for you too to unleash your infinite potential.

For more about Katerina, please visit: KaterinaCozias.com

www.ingramcontent.com/pod-product-compliance
Lightning Source LLC
Chambersburg PA
CBHW050903160426
43194CB00011B/2263